POETRY NOW

EXPRESSIONS IN VERSE

Edited by Kerrie Pateman

First published in Great Britain in 1995 by
POETRY NOW
1-2 Wainman Road, Woodston,
Peterborough, PE2 7BU

All Rights Reserved

Copyright Contributors 1995

SB ISBN 1 85731 685 1

FOREWORD

Although we are a nation of poetry writers we are accused of not reading poetry and not buying poetry books: after many years of listening to the incessant gripes of poetry publishers, I can only assume that the books they publish, in general, are books that most people do not want to read.
Poetry should not be obscure, introverted, and as cryptic as a crossword puzzle: it is the poet's duty to reach out and embrace the world.
The world owes the poet nothing and we should not be expected to dig and delve into a rambling discourse searching for some inner meaning.
The reason we write poetry (and almost all of us do) is because we want to communicate: an ideal; an idea; or a specific feeling. Poetry is as essential in communication, as a letter; a radio; a telephone, and the main criteria for selecting the poems in this anthology is very simple: they communicate.
Faced with hundreds of poems and a limited amount of space, the task of choosing the final poems was difficult and as editor one tries to be as detached as possible (quite often editors can become a barrier in the writer-reader exchange) acting as go between, making the connection, not censoring because of personal taste.
In this anthology over two hundred and ten poems are presented to the reader for their enjoyment.
The poetry is written on all levels; the simple and the complex both having their own appeal.
The success of this collection, and all previous *Poetry Now* anthologies, relies on the fact that there are as many individual readers as there are writers, and in the diversity of styles and forms there really is something to please, excite, and hopefully, inspire everyone who reads the book.

CONTENTS

The Kite	Ian Blacklaw Richardson	1
Apologies	W E Laing	2
Celluloid	Nicola Lorraine Stait	3
Power By Position	Sue Gerrard	4
Hands	Jarvis Mulcahy	5
At Sixteen	Melissa Reeves	6
Planetarium	Laurence Kent	7
Dracula's Daughter	King Brian Boru	8
As Dead As	M Hurn	10
Silence	Ted Herbert	11
Utopia	Rob Williams	12
Wildlife On Fire	P Gilson	13
Harbour Seat	W Mackay	14
Lessons To Be Learnt	James Sherman	15
The Art Of The Watch Maker	Mark Anthony Adamson	16
The Longing	Nicole E Ingleton	17
Inside	Toby Harmer	18
Botanical Market	Dorothy Cowlin	19
From The Clergy House Alfriston	Ray Nurse	20
Some Kind Of Blessing	Ruth Templeton	21
Non Vegetarian Views	Sue Jackson	22
To The Moon	Francesca Greene	23
Magical Manchester Tour	Louise-Emma Barnes	24
Valentine's Past	Joan Woolard	25
Love Is	George Jackson	26
Children Of The Desert	Benjamin Flower	27
Shore To Shore	Steve Richards	28
The Beginning	Stephen Hodkin	29
Friendship: 1934 - 1995	Joan Knight	30
Saying Nothing	Stevo	31
Opencast	Aidan Dove	32
February In Scotland	June Walker	33
The Ebbing Life	Jillian M Moore	34
Rain Dance	David Brinnen	36
Kelburn Tower	Neal Warren	37

The Street Entertainers	John Christopher Cole	38
A Woman	James Edwards	39
George	Jeff Lewis	40
Portrait	Bernard James	41
Hooked On TV	Deborah Joy	42
Protected Dreams	Edith Johnston	43
The Pool	Neil B	44
Truth	Sonia Hall	45
Bus Stop	Andrew Anniwell	46
The Valiant Heart	Iris Pope	47
Respected Men	Yvonne D Gregory	48
Psychology	Raymond Paul Kirby	49
Dawn	W Graham Kirkwood	50
Shipquay Street	John O'Hagan	51
Feather Duster	Tessa Johnston	52
I Loved And Laughed	Lorraine Quinn	53
Such Fools As We	Richard Reeve	54
Engaging Emblem Of Love	Anne Padfield	55
Blue Dragonflies	Christina C Simpson	56
Preoccupation	Gill Powell	57
Tell	Declan McVeigh	58
Modern City Life	Gareth Kershaw	59
Jetstream	Stephen Hogg	60
Familiar Trees	Catherine Bach	61
Sanguine	Gerry Starkey	62
Weave The Mist Of Love Sweet Mystery	Russell McLennan	63
Child	Brian Griffiths	64
Longing	David Frodin	65
The Late Boat	Neil A Mathieson	66
Driven To The Brink	Helen McCarthy	67
Who Will Listen Understand And Believe	Mary Cherry	68
Flowers For All Occasions	David Jones	69
Great Grey Silent Watchmen	Stefan Blackhart	70
End	Frank Spink	71
Sphinx	Keith W Tomey	72

Nervous Breakdown	Monica Sykes	73
The Trickling Stream	Gemma Bowen	74
Cathleen Ni Houlihan	Leon O'Doherty	75
Lying Bleeding	Oliver Luker	76
Mum's The Word	Peter Davies	77
Fighting	Susan Greenhart	79
Untitled	Damian Ward	80
After Thursday Morning	Katherine Ingham	81
Matador!	Guy Statter	82
The Common Grave	Cathy Lewis	83
Footsteps . . .	Yvonne Pirie	84
Gracie Grey	S James	85
Words	Jacqueline Humfrey	86
Empty	Ash Dickinson	87
Serenissima	Kieran Quirke	88
How Could He Forget?	Joan Berriman	89
Distillation	Anne Cooper	90
In The Other Room	Carolyn Wood	91
Innocence Dying	Julie Fouad	92
Society's Band	Sandra J Middleton	93
The Terms Of Enjambment	Thomas Henry Green	94
Fragrance Latent	T M Howe	95
Watching Time	Kathren Eley	96
Daydreams	Charles Thomson	97
Past	M Stewart	98
The Sentinel Tree	Michael G E Demack	99
Happiness	Y Kirby	100
The Other Half Of Me	Jessie Baker	101
Seaside Town, January	Brian Reid	102
Wind Whispers	Cris Clarke	103
A Wembley Dream	Frederick Boyle	104
Magnetic Word	Exley Edwards	106
Past Or Present	Julie Lawley	107
Burning Love	Martin Flanagan	108
Home In Kent	N B Small	109
Le Vivier Sur Mer	Julia Williams	110
Perfection Of Beauty	A Rob	111
Words Don't Come Easy	Rachel Kearton	112

Falling Petals	G T Pollard	113
Bacchus Revisited	George Charnley	114
Spirit	G T Price	115
Destruction's Pathway	J M B Harkens	116
Headlong	P E Medlow	117
Visviva?	Raymond Dinsmore	118
Pressing The Off Button	Mary S Evans	119
Whatever Happened To Wimbledon?	John Downer	120
The National Lottery	Elizabeth Farnham	121
The Lesson	Pamela Young	122
Last Of The Summer Wine	Barbara Carpenter	123
To Glen Corr	P Schofield	124
On Not Seeing Halley's Comet In 1985	Roger Plowden	125
Poetry	Winifred Price	126
Night-Time Twilight Games	Elizabeth Jarrett	127
The Silent Shadows	Vicki Stooke-Vaughan	128
The Second Coming	Ed Blundell	129
Gonks	Adrian Jones	130
The Child Within	Natasha Harratt	131
Thoughts From The Anaesthetic Room	Jessica Fraser	132
The Isobar Stars	Bob Sharp	133
Morning Splendour	M Parnell	134
Why?	Hazel Kearns	135
Hope	Adrian Dowrick	136
The Reed	Thomas Land	137
News Flash	Vivien Bayley	138
March	Doreen Sylvester	139
Stars	Tomas Stanger	140
Road Rage	Karen Hullah	141
Meadow Of Até	Jon Brown	142
I've Been There, You See	Diane Richards	143
Fire Flame Shadows	J Shippam	144
Still Whisper	George Doyle	145
In Solitude	Valerie F Mathew	146
Sleep	Seran Davies	147

Summer	D Godbold	148
Crystal Clarity	Peter Clack	149
Borrowers All	A Hamer	150
Doll Daughter	Geneve Peach	151
Peace	M Barton	152
Light	A T Godwin	153
Suzanne	D Stych	154
Lakeland Mountains	Muriel Ayre	155
The Cry	B Vidovic	156
Lighthouse Bay	Margaret Shaw	157
The Old Man	Bronagh Ireland	158
A Day In The Life Of . . .	Karina Louise Hare	159
Rounding On A Tree	Robert Moore	160
Craigs Broadstone	Paul Hutton	161
Anger	Sarah Atkins	162
Touching The Dance	Helen Baldwin	163
Blackstone	J P Jeffries	164
The Photograph	Rowena Hart	165
Roscof - Alone	Richard Beard	166
Friend In Pain	G Johnston	167
January Afternoon	Thelma Wise	168
Release	Helen Meadows	169
Close	Steve Rickwood	170
Vacant Property	Jim Bowling	171
Blank Page	Alan Jones	172
Paper Birds	Diana Gallimore	173
Untitled	Ally Last	174
The Vampire's Kiss	Y Gregory	175
Thoughts Of A Friend	Margaret Canning	176
The Vastness	Robert F Harrison	177
Revelations	Sandra Birch	178
Pedestrian Thoughts	Mark Corbett	179
Secret Agoraphobic	Deborah R Smith	180
Pop!	Eric Popplewell	181
Untitled	Katy Cawkwell	182
A Silent House	Wayne Barrow	183
Nil	D Edwards	184
Pictures At An Exhibition	Colin N Howard	185

For My Children Not Yet Born	Marty Lurvey	186
Where Are They Now?	John McLaren	187
Body Language	M Sowerby	188
Love	Pauline Newsome	189
Rose	Zoë Restall	190
The Poet	Tony Malissa	191
Wishes	Evelyn Holden	192
The Medium	Tom Ruffles	193
The Dreamer	Edward Harris	194
Seasons	Julie E Hanstock	195
Untitled	Nik Ward	196
625 Lines	Patricia Hunt	197
Rites Of Passage	Rebecca Muir	198
Oh Come Sweet Breeze	Diane Hemp	199
Prize Possession	Ian Brook	200
The Ocean	Deborah	201
Does Happiness Have A Shape?	Barnaby Parsons	202
Insomnia	Alison Gibbs	203
Elegy	L McGhee	204
Shades	Amanda Loh	205
A Rest Is Just A Nightmare	Patrick Hannigan	206
The Burial Of Lily Of Avalon	G Saunders	207
Remembrance	M Lewis	208
Rhythms Of The Mind	Niki Horvath	209
Day	John Murphy	210

THE KITE

He stands alone
on high escarpment,
letting out the string
inch by inch,
until
he touches cloud and sky,
at one with elemental force
to feel the wind
surge round his spirit
riding on the sticks and paper,
defying earth and all that is mundane,
till he forgets he is a man
and in the ecstasy of freedom,
he breaks the cord
that ties him
and soars toward the stars . . .

Ian Blacklaw Richardson

APOLOGIES

Apologies,
Are made of these,
A rose, a wrap, a ribbon,
And apologies,
Just like these,
Adoringly are given.

Apologies,
Are meant to please,
The one I hold so dear,
And apologies,
On bended knees,
Both humble and sincere!

W E Laing

CELLULOID

Whilst the sun began its evening slumber,
I sat coccooned in clannish warmth.
Reflecting.
On work, on life, on nothing,
A child of comfort encased in well being.

A flash caught my eye,
A spurt of human shortcomings.
I sat transfixed.
Hunger, pain and tears lay before me,
A tapestry of suffering,
Embroidered by man.

They said brother kills brother and mothers weep,
Guns rip flesh with no thought of compassion.
All ages are scarred,
Tear track grooves or hate filled furrows.

I sat.
A child of comfort watching,
A child of circumstance.

Nicola Lorraine Stait

POWER BY POSITION

Can't stop, must dash
No time to pause or laugh
A date to keep, a place to be
As a whole new world waits for me.

So much traffic, all red lights
Time to put the world to rights!
But I must fly so go cars go
Or else he'll win, that can't be so.

Home at last and through the door
Five minutes left, no less no more.
I've got the power in my hands
I won't give in despite demands.

Key in the door, here he is,
He certainly won't be expecting this
But the remote control is in my clutch
Coronation Street's mine at a touch.

Sulks nor threats nor football talk
Will make me miss my regular walk
Down cobbled streets with all my friends
It's the one pleasure that never ends.

Sue Gerrard

HANDS

I take a moment in time,
And hold it in my hands.
Then I mould it into shape,
And I place it on the table.
Each moment is special,
One no more than another.
I attend to what is,
And reflect on what is not.
And all the time I am guided.
I am happy to do this,
For this has to be done.

Jarvis Mulcahy

AT SIXTEEN

I can't explain this feeling,
I can't explain how I feel.
Sometimes the feeling is so empty,
Sometimes the feeling so unreal.
That I, a human being of sixteen years earth knowledge,
Cannot find or understand reality.
For what is reality.
I look into a mirror and ask, 'Who are you, do I know you?'
I study myself from all angles (not out of vanity),
I find the same personality, yet a different person.
Could it be that I see the same person but not the personality.
Then I realise that to find it you have to delve deeply into your soul,
Or go through life wearing it like a mask not really knowing who you are.

Sometimes I ask questions:
'Am I walking this path or is the path walking me?'
'Am I jumping or is it the floor that moves?'
'Am I sitting between these four walls or do the walls fall in to surround me?'

Sometimes my feelings run high, happy, ecstatic, sometimes depressive,
But then the answers are clear, I have a love for life,
I don't need drugs or substitutes to make me high,
I feel and experience my life through my learning,
You may not always see it,
It's the most unexplainable feeling that I know,
At sixteen.

Melissa Reeves

PLANETARIUM

Emerging from the dark and spangled hall
Into the sudden blindness of the light,
I struggle to regain my absent thoughts,
        Confused and drifting in infinity.

The sun-warmed bustling London street is home,
Safe from the awesome bleakness of the skies.
The city offers refuge, and I go
        Seeking its comfort in mundanity.

But all the day a thousand nagging pins,
A myriad stars are prickling in my mind,
Goading attention, stirring up my thoughts,
        Posing fraught questions of eternity.

Was all of that created just that we
Might mess and muddle on this petty sphere?
Are others out there lurking, somewhere in the dark,
        Waiting to share our common destiny?

Or is it there to conquer, when driven by the need
In unimagined ages yet to come,
We leave behind our worn and wasted planet
To flee the coldness of our dying sun?

Laurence Kent

DRACULA'S DAUGHTER

Scream
'Til the back of your throat
Runs silent

Scream
'Til the back of your throat
Bleeds

She's come
Crashing through your windows
And stands
Cold and bold
In front of your soul
Knocking upon its door

A creaking sound
Echo's in your ears
A thousand dark secrets
Take flight
Your mortal past
Is in plight

Upon a rush of wind
She's in . . .
Your body flips into a frenzy
Trying to expel this evil
It vomits its insides out
Still aware
Still conscious
You know, it's too late

Suddenly there is calm
As the dawn begins
You draw the curtains
And await in deep sleep
For the darker hours

Your quest now
To kill a thirst
To draw a soul
Into joining
The night lord
And his army
Of converted souls.

King Brian Boru

AS DEAD AS

. . . Uncle Henry
lay there,
as white as a lily
but as dead as
a gutted fish.
He had a half smile
on his wax white face,
and a bit of black dye
on his hair.
Death seemed so silly.
Only a day before
Uncle Henry
Trenchant and raw,
had been wading
through the ferns
with his stone sharp scythe.
I can still hear
its rhythmic swish.
But now,
like it or not,
Uncle Henry
lies there,
as clean as a tear,
but as dead
as a gutted fish.

M Hurn

SILENCE

Sweet medium
Of the spirit's ear
Dark silence
Is the wondrous balm

That floats
The troubled soul so gently
On mystic waters
As becalmed.

And, in the peace
Like falling snow
That settles lightly
In the dell,

A still small voice
Will tell thee all;
Keep thy faith . . .
For all is well!

Ted Herbert

UTOPIA

This place supposed to be a cross between heaven,
and hell, easier to be in heaven if
materially rich, money buys freedom to
do more of what you want, alternatively
one can get very bored lying near a
pool in an exclusive place in South
of France, as an instance.
Been trying to work out what sort of
physiques become actors, super models and
ten million dollar movie females, look so
similar to each other, then Stallone is
the ultimate Italian warrior, perhaps like
Michelangel's David's, endlessly supplying
us with differing versions of the same
films, remade, reheated to give as a glimpse
of rich and poor people, as the twenty
first century starts, only the business men
become billionaires, few of which there
are, I admire their business skills to
achieve this, it goes on and on inside
my brain to try and understand this world
to better the sense I made before,
at times it makes more sense at times
it makes less, a child acts, what caused
the universe of mind and space to
happen in the first place, and what was
there before, only the scientists seem to
hold the key and what numbers shall I enter,
in the lottery on Saturday.

Rob Williams

WILDLIFE ON FIRE

Burning, boozing and looting the jungle
Common place accomplices in the fire zone
With safety matches made unsafe
By their shaking machete blunted hands

Amateurs made amazing
In their heads they are the kings of Kong
Lighting cigarettes
They can do no wrong
As the spark ignites
A small universe begins to die

From a tickle to a lick
The flame sweeps side to side
Then open mouthed and roaring
Devouring the greenery
It begins its journey

Murdering and burning the chimpanzees
And solemn faced animals flee
Some died in the light
Of the faceless fire
And the glimmering ring of cinders
Circled the camp of man
Ready to stab hot fingers
Into the eyes
Of its father.

P Gilson

HARBOUR SEAT

No-one now sits
On the seat above the harbour.

Sunk
In long stemmed grasses
It has gone the way of old seats and old men.

Small waves murmur melodiously along
The old stone quay,
The sea still breaks over
The Scarf Rock,
But The Stephens, The Campbells, and The MacPhersons,
Are no longer here.

Gone also,
The Aurora, The Auricula and The Robert Steele;
Names as buoyant
As the boats
That bore
Them.

Two young fishermen set their creels
Seeking a gleam of hope
Among their catch.

Hope
That in the future
They will watch their sons go to sea,
Listen to the laughter of their grandchildren,
Sit on the seat above the harbour
Dreaming old dreams
In the sun.

W Mackay

LESSONS TO BE LEARNT

In chalk we made our
earliest marks, easily
erased by wind and rain
or simple cloth: then
came book after book
imparting knowledge,
nourishing flesh and bone

The written word we now
know off by heart, fixed,
immovable, permanent as
steel and stone yet with
time and age we know,
profitable though it
be, intellectual laws,
ologies and isms fall
short, the desire for
learning contains flaws

Pale in comparison to
water, fire and the
circle of the moon.

James Sherman

THE ART OF THE WATCH MAKER

Put upon our lives
Like minutes upon the face of time

Imagine one moment the ticking of a clock
That you are the strokes, the starts, the stops
So being such you move be moved by time
One moment half past another five to nine

You are an occasion of the sky
Beauty through form
Torn from me tears I weep I cry
The torment of a changeless sky

The face is still, an absent expression
On which move our hands, the silent aggression
When music stops the stars go out
As dying notes, fading footsteps the fires of love burn out

Tell me colour of a spinning web
Single starlight in the emptiness
Arrested, oh captured by time
Your heart of me not be denied
This the abduction of time
Occasion makes a body fall and die

You only have now, the moment to grasp
Though many hold out God's keeping something back
My hand upon your face, the creeping sky
Wipe your fears, make a desert of your eyes

(Are we) ever the picture, for always the poem line?
I sadden the sea, tire of your eyes
Beauty, I place your love in my ties
The art of the watch maker
God's only crime.

Mark Anthony Adamson

THE LONGING

Days passed by,
The longing.
Yet no-one knew the longing.
Frantic figures flashing by,
Coats flapping on the streets,
Feet tapping out a ritualistic pace,
A face here, a face there.

A face she could want,
The longing.
Yet no-one knew the longing.
Would anyone recognise the longing?
Would they reach out and grab the longing?

A longing, long disguised,
Tears silently spent
No slumber -
Just, the longing.

Nicole E Ingleton

INSIDE

Who knows what lies behind expressionless eyes,
a twisted mind that sees no joy.
Do I cry when no-one else can see,
a silent tear on a bitter face.

A heart blackened by thoughts so grey,
a body wracked with guilt and pain.
Does my blood flow pure and clean,
whilst only vile thoughts remain.

Buy me a silhouette my friend,
let the shadows fall on me.
I'll hide in the dark till it's safe to come out,
when people won't bring hate to me.

Once again my eyes will tell,
tales of times when things were good.
But will they shield the sickening truth,
perhaps as only my eyes could?

Toby Harmer

BOTANICAL MARKET

Do not suppose
that flowers are for fun,
or even to be spokesmen
for dumb lovers,
though that is nearer to the purpose
of the shameless rose,
who with her scent hires anything
on six legs and two wings
to be her go-between.

Some, like the honeysuckle
are more circumspect,
wooing in decent dusk
the more fastidious insect.
Some trap their Pandars
with a painted lip
or treacherous liquid.
Some will give nectar
only to long tongues.
Not one will yield a sip
unless for servicing.
Even the wide eyed daisy
is more mercenary
than you suppose.

Dorothy Cowlin

FROM THE CLERGY HOUSE ALFRISTON

A church spire seen
through blue haze
rising pale
in a pink screen
of light.

Hills just fleeced
with spring grain.
By their dips
for-shortened
here and there.

So differenced
in brightness
and opacity
the green on them.
Such delicate effect.

Ray Nurse

SOME KIND OF BLESSING

We're running wildly with a kite
Which fell to earth. And in the light
With patience we unravel string
Concentration unwavering.
The sky is high there is no sound
The kite is limp and on the ground.

Ruth Templeton

NON VEGETARIAN VIEWS

I've known people who tried it
but, I really can't see the appeal,
what is it that attracts such people
to a so called vegetarian meal.

Why do they give up such things
as a juicy, tenderly grilled steak,
to live like a rabbit on lettuce, etc.
must surely be a mistake!

I can't see any benefit for those
who indulge in pulses and Soya,
if I had to live on these foods
I'd be driven to paranoia.

From the very beginning of time
man survived on a balanced diet,
a caveman deprived of his meat
would have caused a riot!

I find it quite simply amusing
the things that *veggies* eat,
there's no way I'd be converted
I'm much too fond of eating meat.

Sue Jackson

TO THE MOON

O gracious moon, I recollect
How, a year now gone by, up on this hill
I came full of anguish to see you again:
And you hung then above that wood
Just as you do now, making it all alight.
But clouded and wavering from tears
Which gathered on my lashes, to my eyes
Your face appeared, for full of troubles
Was my life: as it is still, in manner no different,
O moon of my delight. And yet I find valuable
The remembering, and reckoning the span
The pain has lasted. O how welcome it is
In youth, when hope has still a length
Of time to run and memory is short,
To remember things past
Even though sad and of an agony that endures!

Francesca Greene

MAGICAL MANCHESTER TOUR

Blindfold that foreign pen pal
Take them on a magical Manchester tour
Let them inhale the fumes
And force them to abide the law
Brown and grey regurgitated again
Perfume can cover up stench
That's what was said by the French.

Manchester has a lot to proclaim
It's multicultural, has a museum, Santa on the town hall
Everyone's second cousin knows Oasis
Life at the Hacienda's a ball
Carnivals, parties and raving all night
But I know someone whose lost a son
So into your jeans you'd best take a gun!

Scarlet and Saffron Dragons down in China Town
Oh the visitors will be exhilarated
Pull a curtain on the child eating glass
We'll all smile on the estate as soon as we're sedated
Cosmopolitan wine bars, expensive couture
Forget about everyone whose always lived here
Take a photo of money; not temazepam and beer.

I truly love this crazy city with all my heart
I know a lot of people share the same view
And although there's struggle Manchester radiates warmth
And when one majestic character criticised it I wanted to sue!
Wherever I travel, whether I become rich or poor
I'll always remember life on the magical Manchester Tour.

Louise-Emma Barnes

VALENTINE'S PAST

My sainted aunt! My mother used to say
When vexed, or My Godfathers!
Not wishing to blaspheme or be thought
Brutal or coarse. It wasn't done
In her day to be forceful except
On the tennis court where she shone,
Poor May. Her brilliance went out soon
After her wedding day, snuffed
By her own dark rejection of another's
Needs, demands she could not,
Would not satisfy - and in denial
Inflicted brutal misery on us all.

Joan Woolard

LOVE IS

Love is like a molten lava,
A fiery passion in life's blood.
A red hot torrent of torment ,
That drowns reason in its flood,
And yet it is a pain
I would so gladly endure,
If only for you and I,
A future it would ensure.

George Jackson

CHILDREN OF THE DESERT

When the children of the desert
from both sides of the wire,
as black narcissus in ragged band
raise bony hands and darkened eyes
to rainless skies,
as withered dust from dust to dust,
and animal bone from ancestors
shared with the grave,
who will comfort thee my native children
of the sand,
where long ago I have been when green
the grass to the stem was high to the thigh,
and yet a promise spoken is a promise kept
as Eden to return to the flesh of the flesh
as the beginning to the end,
and conscience bared and scorched to the blind
as a miracle cast upon a thousand hills,
I will never leave thee again . . .

Benjamin Flower

SHORE TO SHORE

What would they think, Telford and Brunel,
If they could see me now, following in their path?
The modern engineer, so small a cog
In a machine they once drove alone.
Would they still accept the challenge
When one title can link England and France
Or fix a humble washing machine.
Still I will not shame them with despair.
Fame and glory may be things of the past,
But today's satisfactions can be tomorrow's pride.

I remember how it began!
A child looking up at the bridge,
A graceful curve from shore to shore.
He watched it grow, and grew in turn
Until he walked its deck
Exalted above the water yet hidden below mighty towers.
One day it would carry the man on the road to knowledge,
To build a future for himself and others,
So that tomorrow's children would have something to look up to.

But life brings unexpected trials and rewards,
And I find I bridge the gaps in hidden ways.
The miners toil through the crust unseen
Discarding earth to create the void we value.
I use the best that man can make
To preserve this route for generations to come.
But on the way I tunnel through a harder core,
Through barriers man erects against his fellow man,
For without the skill to harness their resources,
That distance shore to shore is too wide to cross.

Steve Richards

THE BEGINNING

The big bang of inspiration,
A shooting star of an idea,
Where the pool of thought was muddied,
The waters are now clear.
The white hot heat of all creation,
And energy of birth,
The precarious manner in which we lead our lives,
Enhances the fragility of earth.
The dawning of a new horizon,
As once sterile wastelands come alive,
And a prevailing air of tolerance,
Ensures diverse philosophies can thrive.
Enjoy the freshness and vitality,
As a new beginning pulls you along,
They blind your vision of the future,
And won't let you see what can go wrong.

Stephen Hodkin

FRIENDSHIP: 1934 - 1995

A group of girls, at college years ago,
Surfaced amongst the snapshots in my drawer.
Then youthful ardour made our faces glow
Scarce troubled yet by threat or fact of war.
Six of us now are eighty, two are dead.
Over the years friendship's maintained a link
Between us, which like Ariadne's thread,
Has steadied me, pulling me from the brink
Of gaping chasms, kept from attempting heights
Alluring but too steep. Still we have shared
Roofs, food and drink, disaster and delights:
Children, careers and husbands unimpaired.
As wife and mother I now seek to fashion
A net of friendship rather than of passion.

Joan Knight

SAYING NOTHING

I'm a leper
When it comes to conversation
I mumble st . . . st . . . stutter and er . . . er . . . hesitate

I'd talk about football
But I tend to dribble or be rather droll
And never achieve my final goal

I'd talk about music
But I sound out of date
Like an old gramophone playing a '78

My tongue's not tied
And I'm far from dumb
But I open my mouth and the words don't . . . come

I always say hello
Well, I mutter hi
Guess I'll put it down to being shy,

    'Speak you mind
     Mind what you say.'

Stevo

OPENCAST

A lavish scene of picture book
Beauty. Rolling green, a static
Waterfall of Almighty brush
And easel. For it, emphatic
Love had the valley folk. So hush,
And reminisce of the land *They* took.

Remember those vast and open fields,
In which God in nature never
Was as apparent - And how
Their wheels as harsh as they could ever
Tread, sped onto lush land, now
A dirty scar revealed.

An opencast mine stands where once
The rambling vegetal vestry
Of vernal magnificence lay.
But no more. Instead, a slag sea
Runs across the valleys to pay
For destruction elsewhere, perchance?

Nature like Christ is sacrificed
For the needs of man. A valiant
Offering, none can but admire.
Loss of the land, while imminent
Benefits await the small shire.
Nature like Christ is sacrificed.

Aidan Dove

FEBRUARY IN SCOTLAND

Jagged peaks of flour
in the distance;
a harshly bright
winter sun,
creating long shadows
from Narnian trees.

A moorhen,
flushed out of canal reeds,
speeds across the surface of the water -
Jesus Christ lizard.

My squeaking shoes -
ingratiating cygnets,
begging for parental attention.

This strange insistence
makes me laugh . . .
transforming Narnia
into 'The Sound of Music'
and I sing . . .

June Walker

THE EBBING LIFE

Life ebbs,
      And still the cooling fan blows on -
          unmoved.
      The bed, caressing your body, lifts
      you gently on its fluid cushion as
      it hums you to lasting sleep.

Life ebbs,
      And corridors, viewed from your window,
      carry the hustle and bustle of hospital life -
      nurses, doctors, cleaners, visitors -
      all unknown and unknowing the drama
          within this room as . . .

Life ebbs,
      The endless parade of trolleys on the ward
          passes by,
      meals, drinks, papers, drugs, drinks and meals again -
      a constant merry-go-round of continuity outside -
          whilst within,

Life ebbs,
      You fight to live or die - I know not which - as
      gasp follows gasp until the interminable pause
      expires into another gasp for life.
      Such effort . . . such work . . .
          whilst,

Life ebbs,
      Your pulse, once strong and even, fluctuates twixt speed and
          nothingness, strength and weakness, whilst,

Life ebbs,
      With darkness comes a blaze of light along the corridors across,
      emphasising the emptiness of life within - so obvious by day.
      I sit and hold your hand -
      remembering the *tea-lady* friend I loved so much before

Life began to ebb,
    Dawn breaks,
    The panting breath weakens,
    Death arrives,
    Heav'n awaits,
    Life has ebbed,
    Yet - *Life Goes On.*

Jillian M Moore

RAIN DANCE

Infinite and unbound
Ignorant of meaning
Unfettered by time
Flowing and shifting
Yet always the same
Patterns within patterns
Endlessly repeated
Twisting and turning
Intense and fragile
Oil on water
A rainbow trapped
In a hall of mirrors

David Brinnen

KELBURN TOWER

I sit on familiar slabs
As drops of grey rain
Drum down
Upon grey head.
The present shifts to the past
Like a disc slipping
From sleeve to hand . . .

I circled my Kelburn Tower
In childhood,
Dodging angry ranks of salt spray
That broke against
A strong body,
Tanned by age.
We played with history,
You, me and the waves.

Warriors under the sky
Standing shoulder to shoulder
Guarding our dark place.
I felt alive.

When daisies crowded Kelburn's feet
I ate bread
Soft with sunlight,
And strutted in happy shadows;
My magnificent earth friend! . . .

We both have aged.
I am the weaker.
My cider face cries a grey tear
That mixes with
The grey rain . . .

Neal Warren

THE STREET ENTERTAINERS

A large crowd had gathered
In the town's shopping centre.
There is nothing like a crowd
For attracting people like me.
I edged forward and there they were.
The street entertainers.
With guitar, bass, sax and drums
We didn't march in with the saints.
We rock 'n' rolled in with them!
Captivated by their sheer enthusiasm
And no little talent
Even the more elderly folk
Enjoyed recapturing younger days.
Then, pleased with such warm response
They took a break to count
The spoils of their labours
And sell their home made tapes
To some enquiring folk,
For they had a business to run.
The sun was warm. The day was young.
A new crowd stood in wait,
And crowds and time meant money
And a day of local fame.
How enriched life is by such folk.
Afterwards, Sainsbury's seemed ever so boring!

John Christopher Cole

A WOMAN

You have your own rough justice
To get you through
You've had your insight sculpted
To see the truth.
You've changed the names of all the girls
Who left you behind
You've cleansed your soul of them
And washed them from your mind

But she's a woman
Her presence fresh each morning
Each day you feel her with you
You wouldn't change it if you could
She's a woman
And just to have her smile your way
Can make each moment seem so good.

You sing her Evening Song
As twilight fails
Her satin voice awakes you
When daylight calls
You long to chase away
The tears that she has cried
She's made you whole again
And cast your pain aside

She's a woman
And every living moment
Just waits to be there with her
To chase the sunlight in her hair
She's a woman
And just like the Lord who made her
You can feel her everywhere,

James Edwards

GEORGE

I went to Brynbach Park,
And there, I saw George, a child,
Sat all alone in the dark
Seventy years old, brain defiled.

I listened to their conversation,
Bronwen, Alwyn and Mair,
While George in bleak isolation,
No flicker, not even a smile

And there the three reminisced,
Oh so many names, that had died,
Then glancing at George through his mist,
I caught in her eye, love, it sighed.

Married for fifty two years,
'it's a job, I wish he could talk,'
Laughter's invisible tears,
'he's sound in himself and he can walk.'

Bronwen's lips rippled with pride,
as the wind caressed *Brynbach* lake,
For the depth of this greatest divide,
She would cross for her George's sake.

Jeff Lewis

PORTRAIT

I drew my brush across the weave
of canvas, and with bold-
ness laid in blue of richest hue
and gleam of sunshine gold.

I took the red of earth and fire
and green of verdant field.
With Artist's passion keen and true
those heavenly features sealed.

Forever glazed in static grace,
memorial to life's span
that reaches fullness all too soon
and sadly passes on.

On my broad canvas for all time,
no heed of creed or race.
And Man may find his only joy
in my sweet model's face.

Bernard James

HOOKED ON TV

One flick of a knob
a touch of a button
the tele's in control
all is quiet while football's on
until Arsenal score a goal

I turn it over
the news is on
it's quiet once again
George Michael's in the news once more
when will this story end

The weather is next
they forecast rain
just what you want to hear
but never mind survival is next
about the life of a deer

A selection of programmes
I have watched
it passed some time away
a tele addict is what I am
my tonic every day.

Deborah Joy

PROTECTED DREAMS

On a razor's edge,
My mind ebbs and flows,
To a dream I have,
Of golden fields, of silver streams;
My dream belongs,
Where they cannot touch it,
Unless I let them of course
But there's little fear of that!

For like everyone worth their salt,
I know self-preservation
That fate charts her own course
That there is never any answers,
If you let your mind deceive
Your heart's beat.

Edith Johnston

THE POOL

Emotions lap on stony self.
Tide rises.
Turmoil. Twists.
Heaves up high.
Hollow fills.
Creating Flux.
No place to flow.
Churns. Thickens.
Destruction within.
Reaching forward.
Forward moves.
Away.
Clutches and clutches.
No reason for this.
Panic sets.
Love help.
Help love.
Steps backward.
Answer within.
Deep deep park.
Seen from outside.
A simple solution.
Need. Want.
Plead for guidance.
Dig free from dirt.
Dilute with tears.
Flow free through made gully.
Back to source.
Empty wound heals.
Scared love the stronger.
Next time . . .

Neil B

TRUTH

Truth!
Sometimes . . . Denied
You hide . . . disguised
by guile and lies?
Clad in veils of mystery.
Betrayed by spiteful cruelty!

Truth . . .
Sometimes . . . Cruel . . .
Words wound and hurt . . .
Bitterly twisting fate,
Allowing them to dissipate,
some essences of purity

Truth . . .
Sometimes . . . Pious . . . Pure.
Will be used, abused . . .
coerced or misconstrued . . .
Diffused by different views . . .
Evading crystal clarity!

Truth . . .
Simple . . . Clear . . .
How shall we find you?
Where?

Sonia Hall

BUS STOP

Bus Stop;
blight, brick umbrella
ragman's mattress,
drunkards lavatory
glassless frame
chip bag cemetery
½ empty Pils bottle
went to someone's head

Bus Stop
view defecting shopping trolley
litter-weave carpet,
spray-can wall
Jo luv's Jake
Skin 'eds rule
½ empty Pils bottle
meant for someone's head

Andrew Anniwell

THE VALIANT HEART

To ride the most tempestuous storm
On life's cruel sea,
With quiet fortitude, so no-one knows
the heart's deep torment.

To carry out the daily task
So those around will not suspect
The pain that lies beneath
A cheerful smile, a kindly thought.

No medal has been cast for this -
the unknown courage.
No citation for public acclaim,
No worldly lure of wealth and fame.

For devotion to duty without a regard
For injured self-pity -
The Valiant Heart.

Iris Pope

RESPECTED MEN

A vixen strolls gently, surveying her route
Protecting her young, majestic and proud
Stops dead, for she hears civilised men
Who curse with disgust her bloodied shroud
'It'd kill my lambs;, growls a respected farmer
It'd kill my hens', replied a distinguished gent
And back they go to their honourable
Duties, visit the vicar, swear to repent.

The lambs are gambolling, hope receding
No point in hoping, no point in pleading
The protected babies are thrown, crying
To their cruel death, vendors buying
With soiled blood-money, the suckling babies saved
From the mother-fox, whose own babies braved
Civilisation, the nature loving
Farmer nurtures his charges, protecting
this living product against liberty
And plans future income, thus selecting
Only animals with saleable genes
Bemoans the laws against his lucrative schemes.

Yvonne D Gregory

PSYCHOLOGY

The word Psychology
Is just a word
But underneath
There lies a labyrinth
Of fears unheard,
Of hopes in dormant cells,
Waiting for the moment to tell
If the time is ripe
To rear their head.
Survey the world outside
The mind and instead
Of lying dormant express themselves
In actions of the mind;
Weak or strong, sympathetic or unkind,
Teach the subconscious truths
Hidden for so long.
Point out the righteous path
Instead of the so blatantly wrong.
Soak in the atmosphere
Of the newly-released from captivity
Experience, from down the years.
Put thoughts and words of comfort
To the often stifled fears
So that all can see the peace that be
The children and the grandchildren
Of Psychology.

Raymond Paul Kirby

DAWN

Sleep brings a blissful release,
Soothes the hurt consciousness dictates.
A haven from the hopeless void.
That anguished awareness creates.

A sanctuary where one can escape
The pangs of internal despair.
Relief from the unrelenting agony,
Reality and one's thoughts must share.

A temporary shelter from desolation,
From feelings of regret and sorrow.
A blessed state of numbed tranquillity;
O that one need not see the morrow.

An unwelcome intruder into merciful oblivion,
Dawn breaks Orpheus's tender spell
And heralds the fearful realisation.
The return of living hell.

Dawn brings darkness into one's soul,
Gloom gathers with the light.
Recalling the heartache and misery,
The wretchedness of one's plight.

Another day with no cause for living,
A constant struggle with one's pain.
O hurry, beloved armour of the night,
That one might sleep again.

W Graham Kirkwood

SHIPQUAY STREET

I'm buying sticky fixtures,
Applying them.
I venially accept the change
And pocket it
Story told to acquire

Constant condensation puts
The mind of the explorer into
The heart of the explored

Now and then
Rough inspiration marches,
Past displays of gimme gimmicks,
An Atlantic blue shower cracks,
Rinsing and dispersing
Only moments ago.

John O'Hagan

FEATHER DUSTER

The child within her weeps for the
arms of love; the hand of friendship
denied: parameters, drawn too
soon leave no escape route for a
cage canary rendered mute
by the muzzled beak of fear - a
voice that would sing, silenced. Wings
clipped, she flutters; falls; flutters; falls.
She *knows* there is another world,
another life beyond the bars -
aches to join in instinctive
harmonies: that barber-shop
quartet of sparrow and cricket,
nightingale, frog. A robin drops
to the sill, inquisitive, pecks,
taps on the pane in neighbourly
greeting, chest puffed with pride
erupts in spontaneous song.
And the breeze breathes easier,
and the leaves clap along,
and the sun dances to the beat . . .
and for an instant, hope, paints
the scene with gold. Robin, sister,
soar high, fly free. Fly free! Soar high!

Tessa Johnston

I LOVED AND LAUGHED

I loved and laughed what for?
As I lay on my growing bed
Remembering my vibrant days
Ready to be snatched away
All for reasons that I loved to live
My life like a colourful rose
That needed to be touched, loved and fed
That's the life I led and chose

I loved and laughed what for?
As I face my box of gloom
Drawing in, smiling
Cursing me for my promiscuous doom
I loved and laughed what for?
For me, that's who
Remember.

Lorraine Quinn

SUCH FOOLS AS WE

Such men those were in dark past days
That gave birth to the building blocks,
Without which no science could come
Nor technology turn that first fine wheel,
And suffering would be most men's lot
Without the knowledge of the plants.

That connection 'tween the fragrant flower
And great relief of disease and pain,
To know that stone placed on stone
Would take man from the cave,
And a glass of sorts would one day
See the stars and galaxies.

So many blocks in every calling
Of mankind's doubtful progress,
And such now familiar ways in life
That now we take for granted,
In our supposed enriched world
We must see that those far back men
Were not such fools as we.

Richard Reeve

ENGAGING EMBLEM OF LOVE

Cold as ice, clear as glass,
The sharply symmetrical
Stabbing silhouette
Of the lustrous jewel
Sparkles like a distant star.

Precious stone, all alone
The facets reflecting light,
Gem Adamantine
Glorious in delight
Is translucently twinkling.

Hard and cold, set in gold
The *Mother Stone* Kimberlite
Out of Africa.
What a beauteous sight
Of courtly carbon crystal.

Solitaire, oh so rare
What powers your points possess.
Binding, brilliant
Your cut, I will caress
Your cleavage in its clasping.

Laudable mineral
Your carats captivating
My heart within his;
So congratulating!
Cubic countenance enduring.

Girls best friend, love defend
On my finger for ever.
Purpose to perform
To tie us together
Exquisite in engagement.

Anne Padfield

BLUE DRAGONFLIES

Sitting by that lily pond
Looking into the cool water's
depth

I saw tiny azure dragonflies
and I thought of all in depth.

        The nightmares of last night
Being ripped from you -
I could not hear you speak
On the telephone or understand
a word you said
I woke up from a fright
Last night.

        And before that my cracking head -
and you could not understand a word I said.
Like an arrow in my skull
The migraine was lancing

In the hot morning sun
The dragonflies reminded
me that another day
had just begun
My fears were unfounded

But I miss you my darling
In the midday sun -
Whilst the azure butterflies dance
My heart flits as if in a trance
I see blue dragonflies.

Christina C Simpson

PREOCCUPATION

Voices are heard, but no one listens.
I guess it doesn't matter.
No-one thinks of anyone else,
their love, their lives, their happiness.
They're all preoccupied with themselves,
and all that they can gain.
The world is burning with hatred and war,
Sadness, illness, hurt and pain.
Thousands are just lonely.
But no-one knows, for no-one cares,
and one day when you need someone,
No-one will be there.
They'll all be preoccupied with themselves,
But I guess it doesn't matter.

Gill Powell

TELL

Come here,
Tell me of pyramids,
Shakin' Stevens, John Wayne.
Tell me of Belfast rules, Antrim,
Those girls you loved so.
Tell me your story,
Though I don't want to hear.
Tell me of Mickey-this and Seamy-that
And the shed he sold you.
Tell me this and laugh
Your whiskey, beer, smoke scratched laugh.
Tell me the answers
To both pub-quizes and life.

You had done it all
But, as the graffiti says
We have much to do.

Declan McVeigh

MODERN CITY LIFE

The thundering crash and screeching smash
of broken gears grinds minds;
the flickering bulbs of bickering light
hoard thieves, steal sight.
All is the sounding beat and stamping feet
of mindless dark, gone berserk.
Here colours stain the night,
sound numbs the brain,
sending the weird creatures of fright
uncontrollably insane.

So an intruder from inside, fresh and young,
who strolls the streets with pride,
soon loses his soul,
though he has only one.

For the humdrum rush and push of greed
leave no place for love,
maybe short term concern,
but 'tis a drifting phase.
So live the city, live and learn
That the mind scar is no mere graze.

Thus with drained body,
a hollow heap,
you need so, so much sleep.
Take it, take your life and sleep,
or else, take this outstretched,
helping hand of mine.

Gareth Kershaw

JETSTREAM

On the lap of night
  A silver needlepoint
    Draws a golden thread
      Across the silken blue
        A precise, hypnotic pace
          A sure, unswerving stitch
            Of double-threaded yarn
              Which tracks the glowing hem
                But when the work is done
                  The needle set to rest
                    This fine embroidered line
                      Is seen to lazily unpick

Stephen Hogg

FAMILIAR TREES

Those are my monsters,
Father, Mother, baby
Striding out across the moving earth,
or maybe both are still and I am moving.
Unclothed in Winter's icy blast, a shame.
For in the Summer's warmth
cosseted around with clothes of green
they seem too cluttered.
But that cannot be, for they are
queened in all their glory then,
And sheep and cattle crumble down
beneath their leafy shade
exhausted by the Summer sun.
Now thanking these great Deities
of mine, who soon cry out for
kind rain to quench their thirsty
roots, and dried up bark, and fading leaves.
And in the soft Summer's light the
clover clouds appear and shed
their feather load.
And these three great trees are thankful
as the sheep that they can still
survive another year.

Catherine Bach

SANGUINE

Oh, yes! I kill . . .
But claim the right,
As prisoner
Of Nature's Law,
To eat my fill
And feed my young
From what I catch
With fang and claw

And if, by chance,
In chicken shed,
Through moonlit dust,
The squawking din
And frenzied dance
Excite me on
To massacre . . .
Is that a sin?

So, what excuse
Will you submit
To justify
Your Genocide
And Life abuse;
Come Reckoning,
Behind whose Law
Will you, then, hide?

Gerry Starkey

WEAVE THE MIST OF LOVE SWEET MYSTERY

Weave the mist of love sweet mystery,
The gentle embrace, soft breath whisper
- Tales of treachery.

Beyond words definition, emotions abound;
Out of the cage - instant reaction.
Now lost beyond words redemption.

Regrets afar and pen to paper,
To fade with time and others distemper,
But not in dreams past encounter.

Russell McLennan

CHILD

I shared a child, at perfect ease
In safety settled on your knees,
Sensed a child, all comprehending,
Shielded by your body bending,
Watched two eyes of deepest blue
Look up with love and trust to you,
Heard you speak, sensed her listen,
Saw the gleam of knowledge glisten,
Saw your lips light up a smile
Which she reflected in a while,
Words, like lilting lullabies,
Slow soothed sweet sleep into her eyes.

Brian Griffiths

LONGING

You the sporting scholar and I the outdoor type
You remain inside me even now.
I am reminded of your greatness as I journey home;
My admiration hidden away with wish, but inability to show it.
In public I am such a man, but at home I sit and cry like a baby,
Punching at the walls with my bare hands.
As I lie alone all that I hear is
The faded accent of time drifting slowly by.
I cry whilst the sun comes up once more.
The things I could not say and tell,
The feelings I can never express.
You will never know just how much I care.

David Frodin

THE LATE BOAT

They stand on the quay, coldly waiting the return
the boat was due back by the set of the sun
their men and their boys were aboard at the start
but their whereabouts now, the sea only knows.
Tara and Kate have a skipper and a cook
as a husband and son on the fishing boat, Jean
they'd set off in the night just three days ago
before the snow and the wind turned the day into night.

They stand on the quay, coldly waiting the return
they've done this before and will do it again
if their men and their boys can make their boat safe
from the westerly storms packing punch after punch.
Jean is the one who stands all alone
her man has the job of tending the engine
her two month old son is wrapped up in clothes
and cries in her arms as the sleet stings his face.

They stand of the quay, coldly waiting the return
of the fishing boat, Jean, hours overdue
the harbour is filled with boats and their crews
and the drinking has started in the bars of the harbour.
Some eyes gaze seaward to catch a first glimpse
of the fishing boat, Jean on her slow homeward trek
whoops of delight and chattering begins
as the fishing boat, Jean appears out of the gloom.

Neil A Mathieson

DRIVEN TO THE BRINK

A threatened species, driven to the brink,
now fights back, habitat all but destroyed
by suburban sprawl.
Man must play God as ever, interfering;
destroying all he loves, the dark side of himself.

But recent records show more sightings of
these shy, light shunning creatures who do much good,
making employment for villagers, attracting tourism.
But, alas, cruel hunters find their hideaways
in ruined castles: secret burial grounds.

Their jaws are adapted for efficient feeding,
we could learn much here
about anticoagulants,
hibernation in cold climates.
They exist simply, in harmony with nature

For them I plead protected status.
Who would deny our children
that sight of black voluminous wings,
streaming out at night like smoky shadows:
dark and bewitching against a gibbous moon?

Their only predator is man.
Be this the night we bring back Homo Vampirus
the sharp fingered, of graceful flight,
and stealthy silent ways.
Avis nocturna,
Of the family Dracula.

Helen McCarthy

WHO WILL LISTEN UNDERSTAND AND BELIEVE

I watched and no-one moved I moved but the
world stood still I waited but no-one came
I was hungry but never fed
I was thirsty but never remembered to drink
I was lonely but never had a friend
I have shelter but my needs are not met
I wanted to sleep but never got enough
I listened but could not hear
I could see but not what I wanted to see
I saw strangers not people I knew
I saw danger but not of my own
It's what people did to each other in and out of the home.
I asked for help but no-one could hear
They could only see themselves in me
How can I tell you what's going on in me if
you want me to be more like you than me.
Oh someone please listen and let me be me this is
the real me not you, you see.
I was created but not by you
I was transformed but not by you
I stopped taking tablets but not for you
I stopped smoking but not for you
So why won't you listen and not surmise? I'm not
like you you're just a disguise
It was Jesus who helped me took my
hand, come this way I understand.
He mentioned my name
Now I can see
Now I can hear but not what others want to hear
All I need is love this will help me to
grow this will help me to learn from others.

Mary Cherry

FLOWERS FOR ALL OCCASIONS

Of course.
Flamboyance and aptitude
For draining and re-arranging
The teeth of all smiles
Mid-chaos.
The soul of heart torn apart
In cracks and reaches
Above the day all voice went away
And the birds tore at
Semi skimmed milk bottle tops.

Now-time colossal downforce on
The guilt switch,
Three dozen
Red missed birthdays
Delivered at the feet.

Nothingness occasions given
In love
And shining post soberly
In heaven.
Passed over by brittle arms
Snapping on a rejection coil,
But focus another and then by
Next Summer
The eyes are in
Neo-bloom. Of course.

David Jones

GREAT GREY SILENT WATCHMAN

Alone, he stands in the swirling autumn mist, watching
Here he stood yesterday, just watching.
All around, wild calls ring out like the cries of souls,
As the mist comes rolling in.

This marsh is his domain, he is the king.
Every day he stands, poised, awaiting the moment,
The fleeting, blinding moment when he will strike.
When he will hurl his dagger into the crystal, frigid water.

Why do you stand alone, gaunt, and immobile?
Why do you stand and watch water so clear
as to reflect your image upon its mirrored surface?
One would suppose you had passed beyond our world, frozen evermore in your stance.

Ah, but see, the eyes aglint, the body stirs,
The fleeting glimpse of quicksilver, a dart abroad in the deep,
The sudden sharp action jerks you from your conscious sleep,
Ready, poised as to spring, you see it.

The neck is stretched, the dagger raised, to deliver death's fatal strike.
Then, a flash of light and a gleam of white, the prey securely held.
Swallowed down the serpent throat, ripples distort the water's crystal coat.

Death, so swift, svelte, the killer strike swiftly dealt.
Great watchman of the marshes, killer, alone for evermore.

Stefan Blackhart

END

It was sudden -

For one lost somewhere on the road,
Radar knocked out by
The speed of it all.

In an end of week hotel,
Such an early object of love
Became only -
That desiccated bitch.

Too tired to shine your dreams together,
What loomed in front
Now miles behind.

Where this lifeline splits -
Another woman, child, world.
Constant dreams have made it solid,
The moment of crossing
Takes place before waking.

You wear yourself
To bone, spinning
The world backwards.
Knowing, you were too slow
To leap, to your salvation.

Now, with someone you don't even know,
In that first moment of drunken hope,
You practice again and again,
The steps which you pray
Will deliver you.

Frank Spink

SPHINX

The soft serenity of your sphinx like smile
        belies this, your raw-red scratching post,
        on this, a bible-black red-letter night.

Readily your open mouth invites me once,
                and once again.

And where we meet,
        in the furry black-cat darkness of the night,
        the moon glistens in the warm damp dewy valley,
        of your silky softly entered, feline niche.
You purr contented, as replete with sweet,
                and sour cream,
One more of your nine lives are lost.
And I track the light of the moon in your eyes.
        And stars.
        And Heaven.

                And *Hell!*

You are the witch - bewitching.
You are the night black cat.
You are the broomstick,
        ridden in the night
                against the moon.
You are Heaven - and the sphinx beguiling,
        and I love you, and your silk soft purrs,
        in that warm damp dewy valley of the night.

Keith W Tomey

NERVOUS BREAKDOWN

Oh to sleep a long deep sleep and wake refreshed, my body free from pain.
Pain, a never ending pain, or so it seems.
A band of iron wrapped tight around my temples
Heavy boulders piled high on top of a cotton wool head
An aching body balancing on wobbly jelly legs.
Mouth dry, no saliva, can't breathe, can't swallow
Perhaps there will be tomorrow.
But, yet again, from restless sleep I wake, another pill to swallow.
No mum to collect the kids from school, instead a *zombie* sits and waits
                                                                                                    at home.
For twelve long months my husband cares for me, willing me on to
                                                                                                    recovery.
Gradually the pain subsides, my body is free - I'm again *Alive*.

Monica Sykes

THE TRICKLING STREAM

The bucket filled from its steady supply.
Drip after drip of liquid pain,
flowing incessantly from sorrow's eyes.

Longing for drought, she fought
back waves of melancholy
only to be enveloped once again.

The plastic cracked and split
from its tremendous burden.
The water ran free, a mere tributary of life.

Gemma Bowen

CATHLEEN NI HOULIHAN

She rests below us graceful in her silence,
Is she finally at rest?
Her rugged beauty has withstood the test of time
and the barbarism of Irish man,
Sleeping harmoniously within her green blanket of optimism,
Stretching out as far as the morning heather,
Cathleen! You've suffered . . . your world . . . your children in divide,
You only wish for trust and a people together,
Centuries of wars and struggles,
Conflicts of interest, conflicts of views,
Killing in the name of God, killing for strength,
Her soft nature we abuse,
Robbed, raped, savaged . . . a woman so timid yet wild,
No more bestowed anger of the growing Irish child,
Endure . . . overcome . . . finally to endeavour,
May the spirit of Cathleen Ni Houlihan,
Be one at peace forever . . .

Leon O'Doherty

LYING BLEEDING

onto corn, rain hustled dust as flies
and the dry stick-shaking day was a sister to me;
'do not begin to think that your words
or that wondrous rhythms can inspire me.

I inspire myself.'

but it is so evening sea silent now
in these eventual looking-glass hours;
remembering once how she, wasteland and lonely as people smiled
and for an instant the whole endless world
was unpeopled, vermilion, dances in flowers . . .

Open your curtains, o you broken ones, you amber old,
and gasp quicksilver at the trembling and broken beauty
of her limbs. See how each we lie bleeding and kissing,
and remember how it felt to fall drifting from skies of
white fire onto organdie softness in each other's arms:

This is how it shall stay. We are in love.

I catch drops with my tongue beneath this ironarching bridge,
and dream slowly of regret. Onto corn, rain hustles wordlessly:

as like dust as flies.

Oliver Luker

MUM'S THE WORD

Was I worth the birth pangs,
Was I worth the dread,
Was I worth protecting
When bombs were overhead?

Were you pleased to have me,
Did you shout with joy,
When you had a daughter,
Or did you want a boy?

Was I plain or pretty,
Was I shy or loud,
Did I make you happy,
Did I make you proud?

Were your dreams all shattered,
Your aspirations blighted,
When you looked at me and thought
You love was unrequited?

Was I too much trouble,
Did I cause you pain,
When I went to London,
When I 'phoned from Spain?

Were you sad and angry,
And worried to the core,
When I married Nigel,
And not the boy next door?

Was your life in tatters,
When Dad went to his grave,
Was I cold and distant,
Instead of warm and brave?

And now you've gone to join him,
Why can I ask, so free,
These questions I could never ask
When you were here with me?

Peter Davies

FIGHTING

I never learned to fight.

Maybe my mother's tales of
War-torn London,
Bombs whistling in the night,
And bed-wetting
And wondering
About morning
Maybe

Or my grandad
Rhythmically scratching
His arm
As though one day
He might tear open the skin
Like so much paper wrapping
To reveal the gift of 1917.
Shrapnel
And nightmare visions.

Or the startled gibbering,
Ducking behind the desk
As the teacher disappeared,
Popping up glassy-eyed,
With the fire truck's retreat,
Body still as still
Ears caught between Math and memory

Maybe this is why I never learned to fight.

When I was ten
Rape and pillage were things the Saxons did, textbook jargon.
Boudicca was a statue on the Embankment;
And Bosnia, the undreamed wet dream of some fledgling madman.

I am teaching my daughter to fight.

Susan Greenhart

UNTITLED

I could have murdered in my office.
Why?
I have over performed for the mentally deformed,
And suffered put downs from the clowns.
And for what?
Only for crummy money.
But there is an annual rise.
How nice.

Damian Ward

AFTER THURSDAY MORNING

And now I sit here in sadness,
as I wonder if, yet again,
I have lost the one whom I want.
Why did you behave towards me so
today?
Why did you treat me with such disdain,
ignoring me, running from me?
Inside of me there are tears;
do you know how you have made me feel?
I wish that you would not be like this,
and that I could smile once more,
safe in the knowledge that you are still
my friend.
Am I to you
what you are to me?
Or are my dreams and expectations
just that bit too high for you?
Something is telling me that this may be so,
and so I sit here, quietly,
writing out my disappointment
over you.

Katherine Ingham

MATADOR!

This body believes in bullying
Because it would like to be a bull.
Forceful in all actions
Dominant over all.

Soon the spear of sneaky weakling
the shallow dancer who pesters
in glittering over dress
which faintly disguises weakness
will penetrate my hulk
in a crafted methodical way
The bull falls from grace
Although grace it never was.

Yet grace I am
Scratching round the waterhole
of my ultimate thirst
Thinking of consequences
and their problems
Forgetting about risk,
a non-option that could
hold the key to the door
that would be beaten down
in angry stampede.

Guy Statter

THE COMMON GRAVE

Lumbering, cavernous,
She watches the dot-dotting expectant
That it will rise and fall
Smooth, rounded.
Strapped in her metal chamber
Curtained, shrouded
Shuddering, shaking, needle scratching
Dot-dotting, lights flashing.

Her form now bulbous, cumbersome
The water cave excavating the unborn mite,
Dark, dripping backbone cracking
Wrenching, corded, cold,
Still,
No heavy exhaling.

Existing briefly entombed,
No baring, caressing, finger touching,
Unregistered to breathe
In your rose filled mound unseen.

In your slumbering earthly common,
But kept,
No ceremonial parting as she washes
Locked away from nature's screaming,
Reject, ejected, ill-formed, ill-timed departing
The binding, suckling pouring relentless.

Curtains opening.
Cases closing.

The twelfth year of longing, one kiss,
Gentle brushing, eyes locking, blankets folding.

In your common grave listen to her weeping not sleeping.

Cathy Lewis

FOOTSTEPS...

Pronounced - Though unsound,
They endlessly pace
The boundary of suspicion.

Quickstepping reason,
To tread lightly,
The shadow of disquiet.

Side-stepping the resound of resistance:
Tapping deftly into confusion, then
Trespass the hall of persuasion.

Subdued shades of denial;
Now in disarray - disturb,
Then fade...

Yvonne Pirie

GRACIE GREY

Gracie Grey spies out
From behind her lace facade;
Her window: a television,
Never to experience ray cathode.

Those rosy days of summer
Are well and truly past:
Withheld in neurone patterns,
Yet love she did not grasp.

Todays' summer lady strolls by:
'That was me! Oh yes it was!'
She draws a reminiscent sigh,
Grieving at her loss.

Decision day never came
And her true lover passed by,
Never to return again:
'How cruel a judge was I?'

No more parties,
No more desirous flesh,
Only emptier days
As they grow less.

S James

WORDS

Moral now there's a cheerful word,
Who talks to *Truth* his faithful friend,
Who talks to *Conscience* I think he heard!
Call the judge *Moral* cries,
It's time for *Truth* his trial's today,
Said *Peace* his playful friend,
Who danced with *Words* and plays with *Time*.
Boredom versus *Happiness*,
Evil charges *Crime*.
His friends are few I think you'll find,
Says *Truth* look to *Conscience* he's your key,
That and *Pride* you and me.
Love and *Peace* come quickly to the rescue,
With pleading eyes, and gentle charms,
Whispering words that cast their spell.
They speak to *Time* who waits on *Life*,
Life's your teacher, you've come to school.

Jacqueline Humfrey

EMPTY

He passed away aged 82
Died peacefully in his sleep
82 years of feelings and experiences
Of struggles and fights
Of joy and despair
Of laughter and tears
Of thoughts he never shared
Of people he loved and who loved he
Of sights he'd seen alone
Of people he'd nurtured and influenced
Not famous or rich but just as precious.
82 years deserving of three column inches
Which we wrap our sweetcorn up in.

Ash Dickinson

SERENISSIMA

On a gentle mist of salt-mud showers,
The clothes stuck to her like a second
Skin; as the white gull days flew
Swiftly past, I made my plans, and
From the top of the Cathedral tower,
I would ask her to be my wife.

She moved like a cloud, a warm sea
Breeze, moving gently through the Cove and
Over the headland to Dungarvan. Her hands,
Such hands! Each fingerprint betraying a
History like an ancient city, possibility and
Possession of a heart so full of love . . .

Serenissima, so close to the centre, the
Flame of true desire as strong as the
Waves that would beat the Wexford coast;
That capable January moon, swathing and
Stirring us from our sleep and into each other's
Arms, nurturing our calmed, perfect spirit.

Kieran Quirke

HOW COULD HE FORGET?

Lived with him for twenty years
Was his darling daughter,
there to wipe away my tears
How could he forget?

Tended me when I was sick
Shared my joy and laughter
Took me every where he went
How could he forget?

When I competed in school games
He was there to cheer me
Even when I didn't win
How could he forget?

An old man now, all on his own
Alzheimer's took him over,
He is still my dear old Dad
How could he forget?

Joan Berriman

DISTILLATION

To catch the quintessential moment of pleasure,
To isolate and preserve it in some measure
Of alcoholic solution;

To catch that moment of pleasure
And to sever for ever
The subsequent pain

Heavens, how I have tried.

But the chaff and the grain grow always together.

Anne Cooper

IN THE OTHER ROOM

Breathing another's stillness
Thinking another's sleep
I occupy myself
Myself is occupied
Pages are turned
Her turn pages
Forgotten paragraphs
Fallen in lost blankets
I reread the sentence
Responsibility is red
The child is mine
Mine is the child's

Carolyn Wood

INNOCENCE DYING

The fingertips of life are showing the way for me
Sun breaks through darkness enlarging life's portrait.
Take me gently, so softly with the clouds ascending,
Take me where life's tears are free to quench me.
Touch me and smell with me the scent of a meadow,
Caressing rose petals as they fall to the ground
Feel life's warmth soothe as it leaves to abandon me,
Everlasting your kiss, touched by pure innocence.

Julie Fouad

SOCIETY'S BAND

Are you strong enough,
To stand,
In society's band.

Or does the band roar,
And you cry out for more.

It's a preaching society,
And the rules,
Are not from the Gold almighty.

Small Gods,
Whipping and stripping,
Society to the bone.

Hard core,
Cry for more.

Sandra J Middleton

THE TERMS OF ENJAMBMENT

The fire runs throbbing
Through my veins
Each tender touch or
Parting kiss returning lust
The fire runs throbbing
Through my veins
Warm loving care or
Problems shared in troubled times
You're insecure and
I can't say three
Little words you
Want to hear I'm
Gender held rely
Instead on acts of love

Thomas Henry Green

FRAGRANCE LATENT

In scented country evenings
    In misty leaf walled walks
When dewdropped branches sway in the breeze
    It's then that I hear your talk

With the silence dampened out
By crystal shimmering shrubs
A god moon's glow enlightens
    New saplings in old tubs

That gravestone is silhouetted
    Where fresh weeds soon will sprout
And mist arising from fresh dug earth
    Quietly seep the aroma out

In heats of humming cabins
    of express trains screaming along
It seems on the dirty green beige seats
    Even there I hear your song

T M Howe

WATCHING TIME

As I sat there watching
As the dead fingers flicked across the screen
Another man shot for his religion
A thousand bodies buried
As I sat there, I looked around the room
At the numb and unshocked faces
As I sat there I felt so sad
Not for the dying but for the numb death
They're so immune to the suffering
They know of pain or so they say
They know of death of the dying day
But for them it had already come.

Kathren Eley

DAYDREAMS

Sitting in my cane chair
relaxing,
away from the strain of the world.
T S Eliot, James Blake, Keats, Dickens,
they all had their dreams.

Reading the words of my
favourite book,
lifting my soul to the sun,
it's wonderful down there
seeing the faces of the children,
so happy with their lives.

Sweet are my memories
of life's great works,
how they compliment
our existence,
breath with the love
of their creators.

They too dreamed,
and in their own way
succeeded,
with their lavish thoughts,
gave everything from their
private worlds.

We too can compliment them,
simply by understanding,
simply by admiring
all that they gave.

Like nature it is easy to admire,
easy to live inside all this
beauty that so many
refuse to believe . . .

Charles Thomson

PAST

Blocked in and shut out
No more no less than this.
The room without a view is in everyone of us
And the room without a view is in you.
Wherever you go and whoever you meet
The feelings they will go too.
They follow and haunt you.
A tenacious grasp on you.
That's the room with no view.

M Stewart

THE SENTINEL TREE

I have been standing here for a while.
I don't know how much longer though -
the grass is moist around my feet.
Summer drought gave me cause for concern
But autumn rain has eased the thirst.

I see the wrought iron work approaching.
Distant men winding their ribboned tar macadam
around the hills. Progressive destruction
threatening those who can only stand, and wait,
and hope that sense may prevail.

My seed has spread with a forlorn future.
The will of procreation is random but sure
until modernity grinds its heel into the earth
which had abounded with fertility
for those reliant on its bounty.

Perhaps spontaneous care will acknowledge
the rings of my age. Protect me from
the ravings of the need for speed and distance.
My horizon remains in bounds,
subject to the whim of the age of combustion.

Michael G E Demack

HAPPINESS

I feel as if I'm just a spectator of life,
Instead of living it for myself.
I'm on the edge, never at its nucleus,
I get bored with all life's trivia,
Things I am told are important.
It's nonsense. A confidence trick
To keep me from the real truth.
What is the truth?
To know the joys and the sadness,
To know the goodness and the badness,
To sample the important things of life,
Refusing the fraudulent substitutes.
To penetrate to the heart of life,
To enjoy patience and vision,
To see the universe as a whole,
To share in it,
To care in it,
That a day may be better for someone else,
Because I am alive in it.
That is true happiness.

Y Kirby

THE OTHER HALF OF ME

I looked into your eyes the moment we met,
And saw your soul, the other half of me.
I loved you then and I love you now,
But I ran scared that day of what I saw,
And you are running still;
And yet you lean on me and worship me,
I am your strength and life and hope -
        But you're not there for me.

I want you more than anything I've ever known
Or thought, or dreamed - so I've run to you.
I feel your joys and sorrows, fears and pain,
From across the world or round the corner,
Your spirit reaches me just the same;
You are a welcome part of me,
I break my own heart trying to walk away,
        From the other half of me.

You curl up to die, but always let me go,
Then send your pain to me across the air,
No matter where I hide, I know.
So I walk back, your spirit free once more
Soaring like an eagle to heaven,
My soul is given wings of joy,
I am whole again, my spirit touching yours,
        Please, be there for me today

Jessie Baker

SEASIDE TOWN, JANUARY

Froths of snow
In freefall flight
Perch on my eyelids
Delicate and light.
Buildings old and new
Face instant siege
As snow floats and falls
Tender and with ease.

On a once green field
Snow drops at its leisure
Causing the horses to bolt
In panic and pleasure.
Lambs that appeared spotless
No longer so white
Abandoned winter trees
Left to their plight.
The ballet and charge
Of bits of fleece
Brought down from heaven
But only on lease.

The white pier arms
Into the waking water
Stroking it gently
Like an only daughter.
The snow touches the sea
And is lost like a kiss,
And touches the stricken mind
Hungry for moments of such bliss.

Brian Reid

WIND WHISPERS

It was only the wind that whispered to me
As I strolled alone in the evening air
It was only the wind that touched my cheek
And stroked my hair
Yes, it was only the wind but yet I knew
Deep in my heart it was you.

It was only the wind that dried my tears
As I walked alone that night
It was only the wind that pressed my hand
And held me tight
It was only the wind I thought, yet knew
Deep in my heart it was you.

It was only the wind that clicked the gate
That left me wondering - can it be?
It was only the wind that opened the gate
And I ran down the path to see
It was not the wind, of course I knew
At last my Darling it was you.

Cris Clarke

A WEMBLEY DREAM

Our football team
Are Wembley bound
Having won all their games
In every round

For fitness our players
Have all past the test
And without any doubt
Are superbly the best

They have beaten the teams
They received in the draw
Some by one goal
And some a few more

Were up for the cup
And tickets are rare
As we save, beg and borrow
To see them play there

When you pass through the styles
And view the vast ground
You decide there and then
It was worth every pound

You glance all round
To find the best view
Glad of your ticket
And not having to queue

The Wembley roar
Is a percussion of sound
When both teams emerge
And enter the ground

The ref blows his whistle
You don't hear for the din
The final has started
May the best team win

Frederick Boyle

MAGNETIC WORD

We are but poor magnetic creatures
        in a rich magnetic world
Where every living thing
        of the sea and mother earth
Has its own surrounding aura,
        its invisible magnetic girth
A mighty powerful cladding
        as a protective shield
To defend our vulnerable inner self,
        the part that we call *Us*
Wherein is stored the knowledge
        of unknown times long passed
Of times and lives we cannot know
        until, as in a dream,
Mind returns once again
        to rejoin the magnetic stream.
Wherein is stored all knowledge
        of an ever changing world
of which we are a minute part
        a tiny segment of a mighty chart.

We see the stars we cannot reach
        but know that every one
Contains its own magnetic field,
        its own protective shield
Through which its neighbours cannot pass.
Indeed those stars are much like us.
        Parts of the living universe.

Exley Edwards

PAST OR PRESENT

Tomorrow is our future
Yesterday was the past
What will the future hold
It comes along so fast
Everything's changing
Nothing stays the same
Today I am nobody
Tomorrow I will have fame
I want the world to slow down
I am forty this year
It doesn't seem five minutes
Since I was in school gear
No one knows what's in store
I think it's better that way
I don't want to know what the future holds
I just want to live each day
What does the future really hold
Will Nostrodamus be right
Will the world come to an end
I hope it's an oversight.

Julie Lawley

BURNING LOVE

I see your face, like an angel from above,
Yet you thrust your sword
Deep within my chest, piercing my heart,
Blood seeping through my shirt.
I yearn to touch your face.
Your skin like cool water on a hot summer's day,
Yet you push me away.
I see you talking to someone else,
My body rushes with blood soaked in pain and fear.
His carefree manner and ease with you.
He knows not of your beauty,
Your engulfing warmth and care.
Yet you caress his mind and stroke his hair.
I wish him dead, his essence gone without your care.

Martin Flanagan

HOME IN KENT

Like searchlights playing
In the trees - so still
The blackbirds lull,
Upon the window-sill
And rippling-waves of lilac
Feed the breeze,
With flying midges,
Butterflies and bees
And squirrels in the Scots Pine
Lightly dance,
As dusk o'ertakes
And brings a winking star,
With dusted jasmine's
Perfume on the breeze.
The moths alight and
Silence yet, the trees.
Quickening, all creatures
That upon the Earth do dwell
Now nod their heads -
Far tolling of the bell.
The spirit of the night appears
With rustling cloak,
Enveloping calm,
Enfolds the lethied oak.

N B Small

LE VIVIER SUR MER

This sandless shingle tricks my sliding feet,
A million sea-shells, crushed by crashing seas,
And those that by some chance remain complete,
Lie, like with like, in wave-formed frequencies.

From sea-grass safety, laughing at my plight,
In taunting play you toss a crab-grenade,
Then turn to face that reach of flickering light,
And listen to the rush of wind's tirade.

I grit my teeth on oysters' eggshell crack,
Remember walrus tears and dry my own.
By wind and moon's decree the tide turns back,
I know this morning's storm will soon be blown.

You see, our love's reflected in those waves,
As moon commands the sea, we are its slaves.

Julia Williams

PERFECTION OF BEAUTY

Thee has the combination of all the qualities that delights the senses and
$\qquad\qquad\qquad\qquad\qquad\qquad\qquad\qquad\qquad\qquad$ pleases one's mind,
You are a very attractive and well formed woman,
Thy possesses the beauty spot,
A small dark coloured patch worn on thy face to mark an adornment,
As foil to your completion.

Is the beauty I see in thee,
Or in my eyeful eyes,
Admirably admirable to have the honour to view a glance and gaze a very
Beauty and attractive sight of thee.

How long did the one of class of spiritual beings that attendant upon god,
Take to make thee?

Thou always admissible to bind your heart with mine,
Are you amongst the finest of beauty to ever walk this planet?

Let us look happily to examine thy beauty and give grace into,
Those looks that set fire to a man's heart!
From whom an hour,
Brings a lover in thy shadow.

Lover's thy have to comfort and despair,
Which likes spirits do suggest thee,
The better spirit is a man right.

A Rob

WORDS DON'T COME EASY

Though you are so close to me
you're still a million miles away
I can see what you're thinking
I only wish you'd say

Words you say don't come easy
as you gently hold my hand
but I see in your starlit eyes
you know I'd understand

I guess our love wasn't that strong
or you'd have no need to stray
I guess you thought I'd forgive you
but love doesn't work that way

No matter how much I love you
no matter how hard I try
I cannot forget your excuses
I cannot accept your lies

So I suppose this is good-bye
I don't want to see you again
I don't need to be a victim
of this suffering pain

I hope you find somebody
to trust you as I once did
but never do what you did to me
cause now of you I'm rid.

Rachel Kearton

FALLING PETALS

The wife's at her sister's, Enid,
while I bury the dog.
It's the last time.
She's gone to a better home
& my legs won't walk out another pet.

Before she's back I'll gloss the frames,
set some seeds; so we'll eat well this summer.

Sometimes when I'm alone I stare at us;
at Blackpool, Southend
& the German rain of London '44.

The missus says there's a time & place for such memories.
I've missed them both.
At my age I should be resting I'm told.
My shape seconds that; but not my head.

But like a rose robbed of petals,
I know I can still find
the woman who caught me so many photos ago.

I haven't aged enough she tells me often -
but I don't want to be just a passenger in a fast car.

G T Pollard

BACCHUS REVISITED

The lock has turned upon the kitchen door,
No more its hallowed precincts must I rove
With feet adhering to the sticky floor,
Nor boil decoctions on the hop-stained stove.

Debarred from culinary privileges
Adapt I must and improvise instead;
To brew my Bacchanalian beverages
I'll commandeer the sturdy garden shed.

From garden tap I'll draw the water bright;
A sink I'll fit to wash the bottles *PET*,
I'll not despair, I'll labour day and night,
Though barred from kitchen I'm not beaten yet.

The midnight oil I'll burn, but not in vain,
I'll labour long to fit my brewery out,
Aeolian power for heaters I'll attain
To hot-ferment my lovely ale and stout.

I'll not disturb the tenor of my ways,
Defeat is not a word I'll countenance;
I've heard it said determination pays -
Except, of course, when spouses look askance.

My friends I'll entertain in generous style;
They will in turn reciprocate I know;
We'll homage do to Bacchus all the while,
And soon restore the beery status quo.

Adversity is merely pleasure's foil,
For pleasure unalloyed would surely cloy;
Achievement's never made except by toil,
Through strife, the more from brewing I'll enjoy.

George Charnley

SPIRIT

A polished pine box drifts down the aisle,
to be married to the fire of destiny,
a shell within a shell, nature upon nature,
the body rots, the spirit is free.

The people mourn for their own destiny,
they wail and beat upon the box with hypocrisy,
they lay their fears deep within it,
but I have no fear, for my eyes see only Spirit.

She is the beauty that rises from decay,
when the flesh withers, its spirits day,
she was emotion sleeping within our lives,
and what the living fail to recognise,
Spirit survives, then carries away beauty,
to fulfil another destiny.

G T Price

DESTRUCTION'S PATHWAY

Animals scatter,
The sound of screams fill the air,
and the stench of death is present.
Chainsaws and axes slice through the helpless trees.

What good is it to cry;
'Save the rain forests'
There is no hope now,
We are on the path of destruction.

J M B Harkens (13)

HEADLONG

Headlong
From danger I fled
Into the world,
Of necessity
To escape the womb.
Thinking the womb a place of weakness,
I dived
Into the light fantastic
And life.

On arrival,
Earlier than expected,
I found no help,
No love,
No warm machine of life
For the chicken person.
No tube of fluid
Or liquid feed
Or milk from my beloved mother.

But in the doctor's eyes,
Before they shut,
I saw money
Spinning like a bandit
Stopping on nothing.

And my life,
the one I thought I'd found,
Disappeared in the closing of an eyelid,
The turning of a head,
The raising of a hand.

No cash.
No life.

Return womb
I want to live.

P E Medlow

VISVIVA?

Summer has come
The fragrant branch is full of blossom
As the lark sings with melodious strain
Her dwelling close against the glean
Delicious berries on her mane
A condescending waterfall sings
To stifle pools extreme
A fleeting swallow darts aloft
Below a white and brawling stream
The dance of the rushes has come
With the ancient orchestra of delicate hues.

Raymond Dinsmore

PRESSING THE OFF BUTTON

The little dot fades to obscurity
and reality is once more around -
No booming noises, flickering pictures,
just a room and no television sound;
only familiar voices of the family
returned to their own problems and joys -
For them the TV is the great escape
from the daily boredom they have found.

When the soap opera episode has ended
is true reality difficult to face?
Or have the lives of all the other people
somehow put family perspective into place?

Once we only had the magic of the fire glow
with vague pictures in soot and flame,
and gathered together at the evening hearth
families talked, shared their lives,
learnt contentment, and accepted that
life is not a 'great escape' game!

Mary S Evans

WHATEVER HAPPENED TO WIMBLEDON?

Venison pate, strawberries and cream,
Gaudy striped blazers which honoured no team.
Panamas, boaters and white flannel trews,
Seated in rows on green canvas pews.

A picturesque tableau with dutiful cast
Forming a backcloth of Wimbledon's past.
Play went unnoticed, being there was the thing,
Midst gentlemen, nobles . . . and maybe a King.

Whatever happened through the years in between
Now its reason for being is the small silver screen.
Our peers are now Stewards and draw up the rules,
Just secondary figures, although of good schools.

Colonels and Captains now judge on dispute,
Applying the rules which all will refute.
The players themselves have become the elite;
Good manners and customs regarded effete.

Now the only courts which matter are those tired and scuffed-up greens
Where stubbled, blousey players reign as short-lived Kings and Queens.

John Downer

THE NATIONAL LOTTERY

The price of dreams,
paid in random numbers,
offers, for a brief while,
the wealth of Croesus.
Avarice fogs reason
when the game of chance is - 'if'
The pointing finger
conjures visions
of what could be,
neglects the odds against,
so mesmerised have we become
by fortune's stake.

Each Saturday
eyes glued to screen,
sweaty fingers clutching
our tickets to nowhere,
we embrace hope, match numbers
then, with a sigh, discard
this week's pot of gold
to dream again another day.

Do our politicians smile indulgently,
hide behind our minds held hostage
in a land of make believe?
Do they grow bold as we replace reality
with this our game of what might be?

Turn off the screen, shut out the news.
The starving and the dying
are playing a different game of lottery.

Elizabeth Farnham

THE LESSON

Sit quite still my little darlings,
storm tossed nights can bring a feast.
When the writhing swirling snowflakes
drift and flail at ghosting trees,
barn doors creak an invitation,
frost free straw and musty grain.
Tiny, squeaking, timid creatures
seeking shelter dart inside.
Tawny eyes look down unblinking.
Wise owls pounce with feathered shroud.

Pamela Young

LAST OF THE SUMMER WINE

Heather clad moors, yellow gorse,
Windswept downland, grey stone walls,
A village nestling in a sheltered valley
With its cosy pub and familiar café.

Three elderly men with a common bond
Of childhood memories, but now retired,
An unlikely trio filling their days
In well-meaning but often unwelcome ways.

An appealing programme
Nostalgic and colourful
With shades of 'Just William'
In its scenario.
Long may the wine continue to flow
Giving my evenings a special warm glow.

Barbara Carpenter

TO GLEN CORR

The court jester took your home away
But your spirit will forever stay
Amongst the eves and every room,
quietly whistling out the tunes
That you gave to the world,
in an all-too-brief stay
Left your mark on our hearts,
before moving away
Became one amongst millions,
in that place where all are equal
Look down and smile, Philip Lynott,
for this world knows no sequel.
Now, as clouds part in reverence
to allow a last goodbye
'Farewell, Glen Corr'
then away past Ireland's Eye.

P Schofield

ON NOT SEEING HALLEY'S COMET IN 1985

Bright Star, would I were confident as some
That I had seen *you* through my telescope
And not the imprint of my grandson's thumb
Or some blur born of alcohol and hope!
Halley! You should be living at this hour!
Your comet needs you, Sir, and so do I!
Dupe of the media's persuasive power,
I nightly peer into a cloudy sky!
Unlike Keats' fabled watcher of the skies
Your comet never swims into my ken.
And I confess my only wild surmise
Turned out to be the lantern on Big Ben.
Meanwhile I stand here getting a stiff neck
Silent upon a roof in Tooting Bec!

Roger Plowden

POETRY

It's more than just a writing role,
It's more a baring of the soul
In imagery
This poetry.

It's what you feel compelled to say, -
But in a special, rhyming way;
You must express,
And, so, impress.

It's more than just the love of words:
It's like the singing of the birds:
They sing their chimes,
You write your rhymes.

It's therapy, it's flow can heal
The hurt that inwardly you feel:
In rhyming shout
It all comes out.

It brings tranquillity of soul;
It makes the wounded ego whole;
It says, with glee -
This verse - it's *me*.

Winifred Price

NIGHT-TIME TWILIGHT GAMES

Tuesday night and I am asleep in my tiny bed.
Cramped so far against the wall, I can smell its musty vapours
as I drift in and out of sleep.
the most poignant of night-time guises is with me again;
That I will allow my body too much freedom, probably arising
from a lapse into fanciful dreaming and love. My legs will be
akimbo and when my knees hit the wall they will shatter and crumble
to the comforts of the inner layers of the bed.
At best I will dream as I did last night, I will be conscious within
my subconscious. I will dream with my soul, floating free,
like beautiful music over an ocean-untainted and wondrous.
Tonight while I dream, I am naked inside a shopping trolley.
Being pushed and pulled at great speed through street after street.
The road is vast and never-ending.
Inside my mind I try to hold onto a piece of music I think I know well,
but it persists in slipping from me-teasing me.
The back of my neck is being tickled. From the corner of my eye
there is something shining and bright angular it changes shape.
Now it is shaped like a ball and its complexion has turned dull.
Pieces of dirty and old newspaper reveal themselves from behind,
and surround me.
Synchronised and precise like sugar on glass,
the pieces of paper land on me then fly free like butterflies.
I awake to find my curtains are still open.

Elizabeth Jarrett

THE SILENT SHADOWS

      Standing motionless, breathing - breathless,
You try to catch a glimpse of life behind,
      Leaving only footprints in a bottomless pit,
Only tunnels inside a desperate mind.

Cautiously stepping into a danger field,
      A minefield of detonating dreams,
You can only see the dark side in front,
      A silent horror movie with endless reams.

Suddenly a dark light falls, covers up that which you covet,
      All is clothed in total darkness, shadowed with a breath of sin,
The silent shadows laugh with a manic vigour,
      The heavenly door opens but you refuse to enter in.

Running on faster until you're falling helpless,
      until a garish nightmare has begun,
The silent shadows flee their corners,
      And the final songs are finally sung.

But I see you back, standing taller, no longer such a desperate figure,
      You had the power to escape them, the will to change night back
                                into day,
No longer considering death and overdosed stupor,
      So the silent shadows are now silenced and there is no more they
                                  dare to say.

Vicki Stooke-Vaughan

THE SECOND COMING

Out of the dark and empty void of space,
Earthbound sped the gentle bringers of peace,
Landing to hysteria and lynching,
Sad victims of a Sci Fi TV show,
Invasion of the monsters from beyond.
Much later when they learned what they had done,
When they deciphered how they'd come in peace,
They buried them as martyrs to the cause,
Of universal love and gentleness,
And when again the ships sank from the sky,
They gathered in their thousands cheering loud,
Not knowing that the warriors brought revenge,
Until the point blank lasers hit the crowd.

Ed Blundell

GONKS

Victoria Wood, past master or past mistress
of true use of words,
slipped gonk into a general conversation.
It fitted beautifully,
with a ring so natural
that's totally unique to her.

A friend from school
was once the supervisor of her sound.
Did he suggest that word? I doubt it very much.
It's simply one she'd heard
and stored away for special moments.
He'd have just recorded it without a thought
with all the rest.

I remarked upon that subtle use of gonk
in general office chat last Friday afternoon.
(We tend to gossip as the week draws to a close).
We're getting on so, yes, they all recalled the gonk,
grew misty-eyed and reminiscent in their varied ways.
They'd missed the subtlety.
None of them would ever use the word the way she did,
for it was but another word to them, a word from other days,
another pointless trend came and went
like hula hoops and Adam Ant.
A word which from those ordinary lips was just a word.
They lacked that special skill to choose the time and place
to give it life again
the way the great Victoria Wood could.

Adrian Jones

THE CHILD WITHIN

I feel lost now, scared now, no identity,
falling, drowning in doubt and insecurity
My reflection tells me nothing
Even my eyes do not betray
The maelstrom of confusion
That is growing day by day.
You tell me that I'm cold
And that I never let you in
But you are blind to the pleading eyes
Of the crying child within.
When I am alone, she is with me,
Her cries of anguish tear my soul.
Haunting me, whispers of the past,
Urging me to take control.
In my dreams, she's there frightened
There is never any peace
Asking me with her pitiful eyes,
Just when the pain will cease
I long to return her innocence
Give her back her childhood dreams
Most of all, I wish with all my heart
That child wasn't me.

Natasha Harratt

THOUGHTS FROM THE ANAESTHETIC ROOM

The hushing ventilation of the theatre corridor,
Mingles with the repetitive droll laughter,
As yet another tiring orderly makes his never
Ending trek up the clog worn path.

Medical staff roll in and out the bloody fort,
Guarded by red lines, white coats.
Theatre greens are donned and discarded,
Like yesterday's news in a last ditch attempt
To keep the outside world at bay.

Who knows the goings on behind the theatre walls?
As yet another unsuspecting victim is wheeled
Through the dark and heavy lead lined doors.
The doors which swing slowly shut.

Barriers within barriers, greens upon greens,
The smell of stale stericol wafts and seeps -
Unseen - through cracks and doors.
The patient lies quietly studying the equipment,
Which decorates their surrounding walls.
As more of their unasked questions go unanswered.

The sterile trolleys lined up like soldiers,
Instruments waiting to be given in order.
Scalpel, scissors, suction, swab.
The patient by this time lying oblivious,
Oblivious to the masked onlookers.

Somewhere on the outside paces, an anxious relative,
Wishing the whole thing was just a bad dream.
A still warm bed lies waiting for its next chosen victim.
Drip stands and ventilators encircle the pillowed shrine,
And time ticks by relentlessly.

Jessica Fraser

THE ISOBAR STARS

I've a favourite programme on telly
it's the one that follows the news,
it's watched by millions of people
and it never fails to amuse.

Its presenters are pleasant and friendly
and their teeth are whiter than white,
but as for predicting the weather
they have problems in getting it right.

I'm told they use a computer
which tells them the weather ahead,
but going by their current performance
it must be electronically dead.

But still I watch in amusement
as they relay a much weathered tale,
when they say there'll be light winds tomorrow
I know it'll be blowing a gale.

Bob Sharp

MORNING SPLENDOUR

As the country-side awakens
In early morning mist
The calling of the song-birds
A sound not to be missed.

Through a cold dull sky
The sunlight peeps
Awakening flowers from their sleep.
A colourful sight, beholds the eye.

A brand-new day's begun
The meadows are 'alive'
With, bees - butterflies and birds
Too beautiful for words.

M Parnell

WHY?

Looking at this mirror wonder what I have done wrong for this to happen to me. This was to be the happiest day of my life for it was to be my wedding day. I don't believe it happen to me everybody said we was perfect for each other but I guess he thinks that we was wrong for each other. I remember when we . . .

We know each other since we was children we play together all the time. As I grew up we got closer so everybody was happy when we said we was get married. I felt that I was the happiest girl in the world. I couldn't wait until the wedding day was here for it was going to be the best day of my life.

I was looking forward to my wedding as each day went by. I didn't think that he was have second thought about the wedding. I think that everything was going perfect for the wedding.

I just don't know how he could break my heart like this if he was have second thought he could have break it off before the wedding. Instead of break it off on the wedding day. When I was going into the church it hurt more that way.

Hazel Kearns

HOPE

He arrives early, joins his crew,
At a time of day when most still sleep.
He starts work on the weekly round,
Picking up rubbish he toils away.
The bags have become lighter over the years,
And the aroma less pungent.
He works on arduously, strangely happy,
As he has an escape,
In the form of numbers on a ticket.
A new escape each week, which lasts till Saturday night.
But on Monday morning he'll be there.
At the depot with his boots, gloves, and dirty clothes.
And the rising sun washes away a shattered dream.
So that a new one can grow, until Saturday.

Adrian Dowrick

THE REED

A poet is only
the reed translating
the boundless, pleading
whine of the wind
into formal song
for the glory of nature.
Kindle the wind
and stir up the storm:
the fiercer the wind blows,
the finer the sound.

Thomas Land

NEWS FLASH

Lord X, a pillar of the establishment,
Known for his good works for Church and State,
A supporter of the National Trust,
His donation of a Turner to the Tate,
Was, at three am., found by police
To have definitely had one over the eight.
He was dancing, dressed in bra and pants
In the region of Lancaster Gate.
Taken to the station at Paddington Green
The sergeant there, commenting on the state
Of Lord X, remarked 'You may be known
As one true Blue, but I would hate
To think the purplish tone of skin reflects
Your reputation. Here you must wait
For your solicitor. A night in jail
Will give you time to contemplate.'

The Dailies then have quite a ball.
They, not court, decree Lord X's fate,

Vivien Bayley

MARCH

Gathering dried leaves
and spades digging worms,
buds slowly opening
no bigger than teaspoons
they are opening
and bags full of leaves
light as clouds.

Noisefully rustling
like a thousand rabbits about here,
flowing over my hands and face
no weight but chill air
slight frost
and an old jackdaw.

Doreen Sylvester

STARS

Black stars cascade the crevasse,
falling into the depths of infinity,
the elders of the tribe
talk to me in native tongue,
they say 'listen up my friend
for it won't be long until the end
and we have a message of hope to send.
Join us now in the forest
where the stars are still above.'
glowing masses cab be seen over the globe
and the moon shines like a neon strobe,
giving light to the people of the night
as they dance around the fire,
projecting an image,
this tranquillity will never last
oh yes, my friend
these are the days of our future past,
and the tribesmen are ghosts
and yesterday's host,
living as one
even though their world is now gone.

Tomas Stanger

ROAD RAGE

The headlights dazzled me through the back window.
The darkness making the road seem eerie,
going through the thirty mile speed zone,
The driver wants desperately to pass me,
Tailgating me, all down the road.
Being so tall up in that lorry,
Does not give you the right, to frighten me.
And believe me, I have come to a decision,
I won't be bullied, by someone like you,
and just think next time you try it,
I want to get home safely tonight too.

Karen Hullah

MEADOW OF ATÉ

This devastating feeling
During my moments of madness, becomes
Numb beauty
On the tightrope edge.

Nebula stars,
Echoes away
Sound aching loneliness
Like amazonian water falling
Into its timeless well.
Echoing.

Reverence paid
For an empty holding
Whilst kneeling and crying.
Salt water pouring
Shoestring arid attachment.
Fraying hemp commitment
Smouldering tundra fire
White snow wilderness
In the meadow of Até.

Jon Brown

I'VE BEEN THERE, YOU SEE

In the beginning it was dark,
The outlook was bleak,
There was no hope,
Just despair.

The days passed, in a blur,
Time had no meaning,
Then events were defined,
Light was creeping in.

There was joy and relief,
With sounds of laughter,
There was no looking back,
I made it through.

You can make it,
I know you can,
It's not easy, I should know,
I've been there, you see.

Diane Richards

FIRE FLAME SHADOWS

Flickering shadows on the night ceiling prancing,
The choreography by the open fire, flames dancing.
The ceiling scene ever prancing,
The fire flames ever dancing.
Watching the ever changing forms as a child,
With young fertile imagination running wild.
Ships would sail the mighty seas,
Nodding flowers fair maidens to appease,
A gallant knight on a fine white charger,
Ghostly shapes looming larger.
Bloody battle fields and lush green meadows,
All formed from young imagination and fire flame shadows.
Now in his twilight years,
The dancing forms hold no fears.
He sees the beautiful female forms he has held,
He sees old advisories with fists he has felled.
Father, mother, brother, sister now all gone,
In ceiling shadows he sees them, everyone.
Fire now only dying embers,
The last fleeting shadows he remembers.
The shadow gazing traveller now this world has left,
Dancing flames and prancing shadows now bereft.

J Shippam

STILL WHISPER

You cannot still a whisper though you
may try, by deed and spoken word, to make it fly.
Still calumny is all abroad, and why?
A whisper takes no part in converse plain
or laughing repartee, it is; though none
will say, a nudge, a fleeting smile of mockery.
Command quiet! Yet the stilled wind will drift
the whisper onwards to ears wide avid.
You cannot still a whisper, nor good, nor bad,
it will be heard far better than a shout,
above the written word.
Cry! Raise the targe 'Allusion' and poise
the halberd 'Fear'! Make fight with
phantom lister, make free with 'Whisper's' ear!
Black 'Whisper' fades to grey against 'Allusion's'
darker shades.
Full routed damnest 'Calumnies' beseech 'Allusion's' grace.
So 'Allusion' the usurper becomes the
erstwhile foe and takes no part in
converse plain or laughing repartee.
You cannot still a whisper, the whisper
still in thee!

George Doyle

IN SOLITUDE

Solitary I gaze with the breeze
Lilting like Pan's flutes
Solemn opus accompaniment upon the moor
Cloaked in purple heather and in abundance
The sky depth dappled in azure blue and flurried
Which an artist would rarely find upon his palette
White Wells alone but proud
With its Roman spa acclaim
This is the scene on Ilkley Moor,
On an August day
Languidly the sun's beams
lending warmth to the bracken and the gentle becks
Glistening with pure crystal images
Furious with supreme force over the rocks
Waterfalls cascading into vapour
Melancholic on Ilkley Moor,
Around a canopy of foliage, space
My nostrils inhaling the pungent fragrance of gorse
The sheep graze quietly and in abandoned silence
Like a delicate web scattered and lost in rugged wealth
On Yorkshire soil, England's cherished zone
Rapturous in solitude on an August day, I stand
The philosopher.

Valerie F Mathew

SLEEP

Light has ceased to be
and the darkness tries to
welcome me.

Soon. My eyes closed but still
seeing. The darkness encloses
me, arms outstretched like a
silent mother.

Stroking my hair and smoothing
the cover, sleep drags me to its
world where light is imprisoned
like a caged animal.

A dream speaks and tries to
understand my full and waking
life. But in vain!

The light has escaped once again
and the dream can no longer harm
me.

Seran Davies

SUMMER

Sitting down on a warm summer's day,
Beside a field of wheat,
Just looking all about me,
Taking in the fresh, smell of a summer's day,

The moment is so lovely,
Feeling the warmth, from the sun,
Giving you a glow from within,
Softly the breeze brushes across my face.

Breathing in the freshness,
Making you believe your one and part of it all,
Nature in its fullness,
Colours and the smells of a summer's day,

A sight to behold, the feeling is electric,
Sitting there waiting and watching all around you.
Birds, and bees and flowers the scent in the air,
Green of all shades, trees, bushes, the grass,
The insects, make their sounds within the grass, and fields,

The naked eye can't see them, yet you can hear them.
The beauty, the sound and smells of summer,
Is there all around you, in the skies and on the ground,
How mind expanding, it all is, just sitting here,
No one in their right mind, could take this all for granted,
This lovely warm, scented summer's day.

D Godbold

CRYSTAL CLARITY

The rising sun consumes
Night's velvet dark
And burns ragged,
Horizontal layers of
Blue morning mist
Into crystal clarity.
The Osprey, spiralling
Effortlessly
On rising air,
Waits for its moment
To extinguish a fish.
Waves wash over sand
And run, whispering,
Back to the sea
With tales of adventure
On dry land.
Your body,
Washed by the sea,
Glistening with clinging droplets
Flashing in the sun's fire,
Invites love.

Peter Clack

BORROWERS ALL

The animating force within
Is borrowed for us to begin
A span of time snatched from eternity.

Each fleeting breath while fresh or stale
We borrow only to exhale -
A tiny cycle in earth's atmosphere.

Our clothes, our food, our body's needs
At last the hungry earth then feeds
Decayed, dissolved, anonymous again.

Our ashes sprinkled all around
Sustain the same life-bearing ground
From where our borrowed bodies once began.

Our home the greedy vultures scan
Possessions scavenge while they can
And argue for all that which they desire,

Jealous for some imagined boon
They also must surrender soon
And let some unknown borrower possess

Whose tenure also is so short
Of what he arrogantly thought.
Life and possessions - everything leasehold.

A Hamer

DOLL DAUGHTER

Oh pretty little doll daughter,
With your dead, artificial
Dolls hair
And your glassy,
Dream filled eyes.
Listen to me
Before the cold breath
Of reality smashes you.

You can't afford
To eat ambrosia.
You can't live on it;
Your sightless blue glass eyes,
Your white china limbs,
Even your gold hair
Will not pay for it.
Besides,
It's not a healthy diet,
It'll junk you up.

Doll daughter
Don't dance away from me,
Stay just another day.
You leave an empty,
Aching space
In my old womb.
Let me take you in my arms
Once more.
Let Momma smash you up
And remould you
So that you're safe,
Safe to use,
So that your pretty eyes
Don't fall out
When you cry.

Geneve Peach

PEACE

When mind is tired and body so,
My strength, will I bring,
And with it Peace.

In the darkest of hours
My light, will I bring,
And with it Peace.

Of fear, or distress,
New hope, will I bring,
And with it Peace.

Come sadness or tear,
Fresh joy, will I bring,
And with it Peace.

Lest ill health, may endure,
All comfort, may I bring,
And with it Peace.

To bring any more,
Would not be just,
Though thoughts of Peace
Are thoughts of Trust.

M Barton

LIGHT

The lace at the window casts an intricate shadow
that fades
as the sky loses its sun

Freshly dark
black roofs turn silver under heavy rain
and through water-washed window panes
I watch objects distort and blur

Fractured walls
fractured people
the solid made insubstantial
variable
vague

I am unsure
strangely uneased
and covet the pillar of your certainty

You speak the clarity of the naked sun
and smile at the kind deceit
of sunlight through frosted glass

Church sure
genetically sure
sure is the strength of love

Yet behind that impartial lens of hot air rising
I see you wavering.

A T Godwin

SUZANNE

Fake a suicide, before I
Produce a love on canvas.

Remain sustained, an image removed
The beauty from a face.

The years are few, the body declines
As lovers refuse to take age.

The oral produces, a pain old and anguished
My part in your future defined.

Step out of the circus, a Paris model
A contemporary look on your face.

Now independence, a woman with name
Suzanne I wish you well.

D Stych

LAKELAND MOUNTAINS

The glaciers made them long ago,
High mountain ranges with valleys below.
All year long the challenge stands,
Come climb and conquer me, if you can.

They stand majestic towering high,
Where rugged peak meets pale blue sky,
Long twisting, twirling paths are seen
Among the trees and foliage green.

From break of day 'til late at night
Attempts are made to scale their height.
First you climb and then you scramble,
Trying out routes from every angle.

If success is yours and you stand on the peak,
You see the whole world below at your feet.
It may have been hard, frightening at times,
But you'll always be glad that you did that climb.

Muriel Ayre

THE CRY

Joyful tears, sad tears,
coursing down cheeks unknown,
like streams or rivers journeying on
and on.
Sobbing, sighing, heart-rending
the cry,
babies, boys, girls, or just seagulls
that fly.
All have cries of their own,
Whether they be infant or fully grown.
Bowed heads that weep and wail,
howling winds flapping the white
sail.
Mother Nature cries silently to
herself.
While the world spins and spirals
within itself.

B Vidovic

LIGHTHOUSE BAY

The sea beneath the lighthouse rock
Swelled with unruffled surface green and deep,
Though heaving here and there as the brute
Crouched in its depths grumbled and turned in its sleep.

Gathering its strength, it reared up high,
Proudly arched like a green glass stallion's neck -
Inside the curve the palest green,
The mane at the edge tamed to a narrow white fleck.

It broke with a savage roar on the sand,
Releasing its mane to hiss in white welter of foam
As it met the suck of the previous wave
Dragging pebbles and sand back to their watery home.

Margaret Shaw

THE OLD MAN

The old man's face was wrinkled
and discoloured with the years
and eyes were dim and lifeless
as he wiped away his tears.

He was thinking of his younger days
when his hours were filled with joy
and each day was a new day
when he was a little boy.

He remembered vaguely his first day at school
when just a lad of four
he had to part with his loving mother
standing crying at the door.
And although his father was the silent type
he was strong in all his ways
and he told his son to enjoy his youth
and not to count the days.

'For life is tough' he added
but just do the best you can
and never count on tomorrows
they do not always work to plan.
And when you have reached your journey's end
you can look back on your life
and remember all the good times
and forget about the strife.

Then he remembered all his father had said
and his eyes they shone like the moon.
For he felt the touch of his mother and father
and he knew he would be joining them soon.

Bronagh Ireland

A DAY IN THE LIFE OF . . .

He casually lights up his expensive cigar,
Drives to work in his flashy new car.
She lights a fire to keep her warm,
Walking barefoot, with a child on her arm.
He buys a suit for a business meeting,
Conran, Armani, Klien or Keating?
She carries a bin-bag of her only clothes,
Ragged and dirty, full of holes.
He goes home, pours a Vodka on ice,
Another cigar would be quite nice!
She tries to sleep, cold and afraid -
Is she safe, where she has laid?

His alarm wakes him up at precisely eight,
Flight to Barbados - mustn't be late.
They lift her up, carry her body away,
They don't show emotion, it happens each day.

Karina Louise Hare

ROUNDING ON A TREE

Floats the sun in tethered cooling,
Low in a snaked bow's crook
Despairing of our wayward adoration.

Mute star meet for whispers.
In retreat unbrazen, cowed.
A desert god in frosted mood.

And we most distanced,
Parched by this ghost of heat
Seem for one culled moment
Utterly between
The certain and the infinite.

Who now dispute the sainthood of our longing?
Irritant that bears not pearl but flint, blunt
Raw as winter underfoot.

Ice measures: heat explores.
Against the frost our tongue dance doubles,
Flamed to chorus: hell's garland
Threading the told tale,
Healing bruise of truth.

Uneasy in the shudder of hills,
In wind's sobriety. No ease
To lay the bitterness of earth's
And our velocity.

For come we,
As a hare rounding on a tree
At evening, in the corpse light.

Robert Moore

CRAIGS BROADSTONE

A blanket of bog
Drapes over a plateau
Known as the Long Mountain,
And upon it near Finvoy
A three chambered court cairn
Lies sleeping;
Dreaming of the visitors
The rituals and the burials,
And whatever else it may have witnessed
In five thousand years or so.
And though now protected
By the law of the land,
The locals have often took care of it.
When the great capstone fell about 1833
The men of the townland replaced it,
They brought up railway sleepers from Ballymoney
Made a staircase
Then eased the stone up.
These men have long since fallen too
But what they had worked for that week
Is still standing.
And this place and everything around it
Should remind us once again
Of what little time we have been given;
For we are but the white silky hair
Upon the cotton grass,
That is borne away
On a midsummer wind,
And scattered
Both near and far.

Paul Hutton

ANGER

She is angry with you
You stare at a sky dripping red
Like a child's painting,
And wonder
What word was it, or look or gesture
That had you tried and found guilty
Before you realised it?
She loves you
She said so
And you try to reconcile the two
The sky's crazy pattern
Mirrors your thoughts.
She is disappointed in you.
She expected so much,
Too much?
The sun is setting,
Will it set on
Your anger
Your hurt
or
Your love?

Sarah Atkins

TOUCHING THE DANCE

On the inside
I am graceful
A dancer
Light-footed, perfect,
Perfectly formed,
Clothed in a perfectly fitting
Beautiful, gauzy, floating
Set of veils.
My every movement is
Graceful and poised
In the right place
Just what it is, no more, no less -
But on the inside,
The dancer
Is only a tiny dancer
Dancing in her own tiny space
Round in a circle
Round and round.
If I can greet
My dancer
And touch her hand,
She will carry me into a dance
Larger and larger
To the outside
And out of the outside
Down paths she has never trodden.

Helen Baldwin

BLACKSTONE

Deep within the Earth's
Warm soul,
We enter through
A man made hole.

Down beneath the
Blackstone lie,
Where you work
Until you die.

To swallow dust
Consume the earth,
Expected from the
Time of birth.

Down beneath the
Blackstone lie,
Where you work
Until you die.

We will know who
Oils the gate,
When we enter in
Our wooden crate.

Down beneath the
Blackstone lie,
Chiselled words
In stone I cried.

J P Jeffries

THE PHOTOGRAPH

Your eyes,
Bright as an angel's,
Yet twice as pure.
Standing by the cold fireplace,
In all your splendour.
Scattering your desperate nobility
Like confetti at your wedding.
Your body,
As strong as the wall on which you lean,
Hiding beneath your glamour you try not to be seen.

But I can see the shy man,
Hidden away like an untold secret.
That was really you - your truth,
Not this photograph - your lie,
Not this ugly masquerade.
Once you would have shied from a camera
So what is this I see?
Only some desperate photographer's ideality.

Oh I know you so well,
I insist, I insist I did.
You may disagree,
But I would remind you and remind you,
And never tire from my folly
I can still see your eyes,
Bright as an angel's,
Yet twice as pure.
I can see through the walls you have built,
I can tear them down and find your guilt.

Rowena Hart

ROSCOF - ALONE

Waves lap upon the shore, who could ask for more
than this?
Sandpipers by the score, can you see? Running fast
close by.
Wind-surfer skimming gracefully till gust upsets
his dignity.
Erect again the sail is set, away he glides
to yet another splash
The breeze still rustles through the leaves, gently
trying to appease, for the surfer's hash.
Alas, I have to smile, the pride and joy can only
last a while, till once again into the brine.
Whose eyes but mine are here to see? Whose ears
to listen carefully?
I am alone again, there is no one else but me,
To smell the brine and taste the salt, not to forget
the sand upon my face.
Oh cripes! A powered ski-boat roaring by! I'm
off again to more gentle pace.

Richard Beard

FRIEND IN PAIN

I stand on the outside,
Desperately seeking a cavity into which I may crawl,
Raging and fighting, against nothing, but all,

I have movement, but motionless slowly sneaks in,
As I stop and watch you gently withdraw,
Biding an escape to a shell, made from within,

I'm feeling your pain as if I were you, I know you
Lie lonely, longing to sleep,
But your wish goes ungranted, as the night passes through,
No ease do you feel, still you're compelled to cry.

Freely you gave to a God given cause,
Your sin was love as never before,
Your sight has become blindness from the hurt of your cries,
As you reach to touch nothing, you scream out aloud,
Yet again you fall slowly, wounded by truth,
I stand in your shadow,
Not knowing how to get through, just hoping
You know that whilst these walls
Still surround you,
I'm here for you.

G Johnston

JANUARY AFTERNOON

Small planes in the sky over the bleak January airfield
Lights at nose and wing-tip pin-pointed in the dull afternoon light
Landing one after the other on the grassy strip
So many people learning to fly on a dull winter day.
Other planes near at hand, revving, taxiing, waiting
for their turn to take off.
The grandchildren excited at first, then getting bored, cold
The museum they had wanted to see closed until April.
'Can we go into the cafe now' they clamour. January afternoon

Thelma Wise

RELEASE

The wind blows through my hair
as I raise my head to the sky
a thousand troubled thoughts
form a whirlwind in my mind.

I offer my hands to the heavens
and let the force carry me away
my mind releases the pain
that's been inside for all this time.

I close my eyes and lay back
letting the sun lap at my face
as the worries of a lifetime
subside leaving only peace.

I rise dizzy from the heat
and dance like a child
through the flowers before me
ripping daisy chains from my neck.

Free as a bird I fly
from the menacing cliffs above
carried by the wind,
I turn to meet my maker.

Helen Meadows

CLOSE

Heartbeat intense I remember that African sky
The light of day is now passing me by
The more I run the thoughts through my head
The more I think I'll confess but I hesitate -
It's so hard to breathe when I feel I'm going to suffocate.

Looking from the end of the garden
I see the black pitching so violently.
A premonition of passion before the cloud's shadow.
Chain lightening flashing before me like my
Life story at a terrifying rate -
I turn and retreat from the open gate.

I couldn't stick it out it was too much
My rational thoughts are right out of touch.
I daren't even hope with your quiet indecision
Which tears me apart with utmost precision
So I look back and face this awesome vision.

I saw the evil sky moving in on me
Tighter focus, overpowering and seizing me.
Affecting a mood I'm trying to escape
It's what I learnt to love and hope to hate
Before the sky opens and my chains break.

Madly and deeply I sat and dreamt
About what I said and what I meant,
Humid air closing in on my soul
Losing my grip losing control.
The heart and love are in the guiding hand of fate
And I turn and close the garden gate.

It's so hard to breathe when I feel I'm going to suffocate.

Steve Rickwood

VACANT PROPERTY

Old.
Ancient.
Tired, decrepid.
Broken, worn out
Lost.

Photograph.
Memories.
Faded, crumpled.
Taken, discarded.
Forgotten.

Friendships
Forged, forsaken.
Ruined, stolen.
Torn.
Shredded.

Silence
Endless, empty.
Spurned, rejected.
Abandoned, abhorrent.
Alone.

Bitterness, hatred.
Resentment, redundant.
Thoughts.
Words.
Deeds.

Spoiled.
Soiled.
Tarnished.
Tainted.
Ended.

Jim Bowling

BLANK PAGE

Clean, white with lines all bare
glaring defiantly
as though I'm not there

No offers of criticism, wit or pretence
you just sit there
with plain indifference

I'm lost for ideas, I can't really think
I keep racking my brains
I can't sleep a wink

So come on little note pad
don't be a snob
if it wasn't for me
you'd be out of a job.

Alan Jones

PAPER BIRDS

Coasting by neighbours' fences
Go shapes with printed wings
Swan-folded brittle softnesses
In my imaginings.

Newspaper birds are gusted
Far on with yesterday;
Pretended flaps and make-believe
Must serve for their ballet.

Crumpled-up remainders
Of headlines that once shone;
Untidy haberdasheries
On tides that aren't their own.

Their titles tatters; bills all dumb
With nothing left to say:
Poor things in gutter barricades
They cannot fly away.

Diana Gallimore

UNTITLED

You won it, now take it.
It's already yours.
Go off and be happy
You've got that reward.

Don't stop to thank parents,
Producers and cast
You've got what you needed
The flag's at half mast.

Just trample those people
You've loathed all your life
By killing the dead ones
Your pleasure is rife

You crave to be feared
But you're lower than low.
Don't tell us a thing
We already know.

Currently touring 'Round you own ego'.

Ally Last

THE VAMPIRE'S KISS

As I lay in bed one night,
I saw a silhouette,
standing just before my bed,
whom I had never met.

I felt like I was in a trance,
dark eyes bore into me.
I felt a coldness in the air,
and sensed his mystery.

A handsome figure dressed in black,
a man to hold me tight.
So why as he stood very close,
was I so full of fright.

The dark eyes still were holding mine,
I could not look away.
I could not help to feel inside,
darkness would turn to day.

Those eyes then took away my doubt.
Why did I feel like this?
As ecstasy withheld my thoughts,
I felt the vampire's kiss.

Y Gregory

THOUGHTS OF A FRIEND

They said I would see it,
It would be big and bright,
Then I was to follow it,
Go in to the light.

They said I'd feel no pain,
Would not have to fear,
The pain is still so very great,
Yet I know the light is near.

I was told to prepare for it,
I guess I thought I had,
Shed all my tears and I thought
I'd no longer be sad.

All the things I wish I hadn't,
Ever said or done,
Now no way of changing them,
Because my time has come.

Perhaps if I close my eyes,
The light I will not see,
It's shining bright, won't go away,
I know it's come for me.

I want to live,
Does no one care,
The light is coming,
It is not fair.

I'm walking now in to the light,
No longer able to put up a fight,
The pain has gone and I have no fear,
I'm happy now so don't shed a tear.

Margaret Canning

THE VASTNESS

ah life; there is so much irony,
in the rising of the sun,
in the death agony,
of tired life-forms being reborn,
into the new life; out of the old,
coming to the warmth; from out of the cold,
of this lonely existence; that so often is,
mine for so long; the most of my life,
just for that touch of a lover's kiss,
to ease the soreness; of a lost romantic's soul,
an odd sort of curse,
for what else could I be; in this vast,
wilderness; that is; our universe,
and sure it makes me feel small,
seeing how I stand in comparison,
somewhere in the midst of it all,
all the never-ending glory,
that is this infinite quest,
this statement for the gods on high,
or below; or around me; or in the depths of the sea,
or the bowels of the earth; and also; the sky,
or likewise,
seen in the mirror; through these eyes,
where the vastness is mirrored back.

Robert F Harrison

REVELATIONS

I sit here and talk -
And you just stare,
Me over here -
And you over there.
I inwardly tremble,
And outwardly shake,
With every small utterance
And new confession I make.
Telling my life's history, I wonder?
Revealing myself too much?
But our minds are so far apart,
So far out of touch:
I fear I'll reveal my weaknesses
And you may destroy me.
But I know you are here to help,
And you are not, my enemy.

Sandra Birch

PEDESTRIAN THOUGHTS

Sometimes I wonder who I am,
And who I should be.
Or when people look at me,
What they can see.
If the shoe fits it should be worn,
But after a while I grow out of it.
I often move from shoe to shoe,
Trying them for size,
Looking for somewhere to put my life.
I tend to envy those I meet,
Who wear their shoes,
While I stand with bare feet.
Now I can see things in a different way,
The shoes I've got are here to stay.
Even though they're ragged the world won't end,
It's nothing a little polish can't mend.

Mark Corbett

SECRET AGORAPHOBIC

My mind is at war
With itself.
An insuperable fear has smothered
All sense or reason.
A once dormant volcano erupted
Onto my unsuspecting world,
Its infernal embers smoulder still
And in a Plutonic frenzy
Ignites my imagination so that
My heart thumps as if to leap
From my breast.
I cannot swallow or catch my breath
As if to suffocate on fear.
What is it?
Where did it come from?
Why me?
Too afraid to tell,
Too wary of scathing remarks
From friends who think
They know me
So well.

Deborah R Smith

POP!

Given this nickname like my father before me
The old English river popples and spits
Then Latin hits the bubbling boys with
Populous, populace, popular, pop
Their fizzy music and afterlife, when high and low blur
Blown up like young Toad with Brillo boxes and soaps
The culture at the end of the modern
The familiar made strange.

Eric Popplewell

UNTITLED

sometimes the country sun shines shallow
longing won't fade when darkness comes
light is mocking, time is slipping
screaming space for the one I wish, yet not there

to deny is to wound the stony earth
to hope again, to die another death
would that I might just fall
embrace a stagnant pool of ignorance in the trees

I run and falter and scrabble but inescapably conscious
it has me gripped: the eternal spring
of just a word, just a creamy note
not there, and I bow shadow-wards in pain

Katy Cawkwell

A SILENT HOUSE

Within a silent house in the stillness of night
A log fire fades and burns away life
Alone he sits overwhelmed by thoughts
They circle his mind
With an unshakeable force

There's movement abound
But there's nothing to see
A ghost runs from silent screams
A disciple of the darkest dreams
And as he tries to escape Time's heartbeat
The staircase creaks beneath no one's feet

Through the windows, past the trees
On display for no one to see
Is the broken ghost of empty dreams
He's locked in a world where he cannot be heard
Made to pay for the days
When he let the moment pass
And he walked away

Now the curtains cast strange pictures
Upon his closed eyes
The shadows pass like spiders
Creeping across the sky

All life is ceased by a silent sword
But through the rain and thunder
There's an aching cruel wonder
At the eternal silence of God

Wayne Barrow

NIL

It was in Leeds,
and he
looked at
my
De Niro videos and
my
Dostoeyovsky books and
my Dylan records.

I made him coffee in
my
room and talked about
Argos and a car
repayment scheme.

And he talked about
a
dead wife and about
a
magical baby son and about
a
job at a paper mill.

And I
sat and listened
in my room,
feeling
curiously
ashamed.

D Edwards

PICTURES AT AN EXHIBITION

Autumnal shades and shadows bleed,
Where gold and silver birches stretch,
Encompassing primeval need -
Live, die, decay for heather moors.

Dark water through the mill will stream,
Daily tasks will not divert.
Nearby lovers embrace and dream,
Cool water sounds in memory.

A country house of mellow years,
Appreciates as seasons change,
With gardens full of flowers, not tears,
And loses not her bright image.

The tilt and rock *cheval de bois*
With bright paint work and twirling brass,
Gives children more than *blanc et noir*
But colours various and noise.

Fires of colour, sky at night
Above the city traffic roar,
Contrasts strangely with the pools,
And dragon flies of glass and light.

Colin N Howard

FOR MY CHILDREN NOT YET BORN

Supple and more golden then
I leapt from hill to hill
In the green hours of morning
On through the haze of day
Into the blue bygone hours
of an evening horizoned
and red licked in its dying.

My world then was not an oyster
But the soft shell of tufted grass
Where the Heathen laid his head
as the heather sang
and the song drowned out
The distant rumble of years to come.

Peace flew then
In the feathers of the fortunate birds
Flying higher even
than the sound of their own cries.

Someday I shall take my children there,
They warm wombed now,
in the mother to come
Look of my lover's eyes.

And there amongst
The crumbling crusts
of those ancient boundary walls
Where the wind blew troubles to dust,
we shall listen to the lapping
of the wind blown heather
And for a moment,
The distant rumble of their coming years
Shall be stilled.

Marty Lurvey

WHERE ARE THEY NOW?

Here you are sitting alone!
Where are they now?
Where have they gone?
They are here when they need you,
And are gone when they don't.

Who are they and what do they want?
Miracle cures or blood from a stone?
Draining you dry, emotionally torn?
But when they don't need you,
Where have they gone?

You are tired and weak, and
They take even more;
But you cannot refuse them,
... Well ... not anymore.

You are weak and depressed, and
They want even more;
They continue to drain you,
... I ...can't take anymore!

Why do they take?
Where do they go?
Why don't they stay
When I'm feeling low?

Why don't they help me?
Do they forget?
Why can't they see,
I may need them yet?

Why don't they listen?
Should I demand that they tell?
Will they tell me a thing?
No chance in Hell!

John McLaren

BODY LANGUAGE

Nibbled nails, sure sign.
Constantly fingering flute of wine.
Cushions hugged closer, than close
Fingers, unwittingly profile the nose

Silver chain links countlessly felt.
Occupied fiddling buckle on belt.
Hand clenched, palms moist,
Caressing lips unknowingly pursed.

Battered beer-mats, survivors of a battle
Involuntary cough, husky rattle
All unguarded revealing moments of secret strife,
Valuable, important process of life.

M Sowerby

LOVE

Is it so wrong to want love
If only in the heart of my imagination?
Is it so wrong to feel pain so joyous
       that condemns the longing for what can never be?
To grab a chance of happiness
If only for a moment
Is worth a life of memories to behold -
Such memories as can never e'er be taken
From the dreams and yearning deep inside of me.

Pauline Newsome

ROSE

Sweet aroma
Delicate fragrance
She taunts
Virginal white
Priceless finery
Softly alluring touch
She blesses

Zoë Restall

THE POET

What is a poet?
He is a deep thinking person
who puts all his thoughts and feelings down on paper
to share with everyone who wants to!

He tells tales
of youth and love mis-spent,
Dreams and hopes that have been dashed in life
And old age that stealthily crept forward to replace them.

He woos young maidens
with love and romance,
That flows from his very being
with such ease and grace.

The pen they say is mightier than the sword
but it too can wound
If care is not taken
when things are written about people.

When a poet passes from this earth
a great sorrow is felt by everyone who knew them,
No more poems of love and hope
only teardrops and heartaches will remain.

So farewell poet of love and understanding
whose words are beyond poor mortal man
But I'm afraid to say
even they fade and pass away some day.

Tony Malissa

WISHES

Are on pieces of paper,
Fragments of dreams.

Are for no more tears,
And smaller the pain.

Are glimpses of brilliance,
Curse to the empty page.

Are the shadows of smiles,
The change in the light.

Are the wonder of constancy,
Caught in the memory of flight.

Evelyn Holden

THE MEDIUM

The air is stale, unmoving, somnolent
The circle rests between sessions
Phenomena there have been in abundance
And a feeling of mutual congratulation
Hangs pall-like

Lights down

Dressed in black the star
Throws back her head and moans
All lean forward
We are off again . . .
A glow from the cabinet
Was that a face? Surely yes
Though eyes strain to pick out patterns
The voice, low, husky, hard to hear
Words half lost in the carpet dust

But the messages mean so much to everybody
Many are called, all are chosen

Tom Ruffles

THE DREAMER

To live is to dream and wish,
To want and need and seek,
For the dreamer holds the key,
To being humble, kind and meek.

The dreamer is the inventor,
Of machine and chemical mix,
Experimenting on our behalf;
Unmasking life's tricks.

They mock the dreamer now,
But in time they'll know the answer.
Millions have but one dream;
A world without cancer.

Edward Harris

SEASONS

Spring, the child is born
Young, strong, beautiful
He reaches to the sun
For comfort, for life.
Summer, the young man smiles,
The warmth clothes his body,
He runs, gallops.
The days are long,
Strong, he grasps at life.
Autumn, the man looks up,
Golden leaves, golden sky,
He wonders at the season's beauty,
Days are shortening, time is slowing,
Winter, the old man's time.
Stumbling, plodding.
Endless nights, darkening days,
Slowly the year ends,
The seasons die.

Julie E Hanstock

UNTITLED

Like a tiger running through the rain forest,
We chased the day, butterflies in the wind.
Along the sandy shore in and out the waves,
But it flew so fast we could never catch it.

That day we lost our fantasy.

Over the wall like silver rain, it splashed through the
Graveyard,
We gave hot pursuit but the gravestones found our feet.
Trees in a forest, they grew all around us,
And for a moment we were lost in their lives and memories.
Trundling through the Second World War and the Titanic,
We shot out the other side like bullets.
Onto the white washed cliffs,
But the sky turned grey on our small bodies as we saw it
Swim out to sea.
We lurched in the waves and choked on the sand.
And felt time dragging on our feet in strands of seaweed.
We swallowed salty mouthfuls as we reached for the light,
And gasped the stale air with hungry lungs.
We escaped but I sometimes think we should have stayed,
On that shore cut off by the tide;
The day we lost our fantasy.

Nik Ward

625 LINES

Fed on a diet of mediocrity
The mind remains a dry sponge,
Unstretched, waiting.
Trivia adsorbed,
Evaporating.
Nothing absorbed,
Untouched, waiting.
A lethargic finger reaches out,
Presses the remote control button;
Mindlessly waiting.

Patricia Hunt

RITES OF PASSAGE

Cracking mirror cannot hide
Unrelenting mask to wear
Pummelled by pernicious pride
Suppressed primal force to tear

Amber lava to abate
Vanquished veins of viscous flow
Soporific deviate
Surging current; embered glow

Shackles melt in wild embrace
Fire to purge and time to cease
Molten to emancipate
Run to free and free release

Ride the tide; surrealist trance
Swathing dreams to ebb and flow
Throbbing rhythm; tribal dance
Soaring high; serene below

Dragging down and down once more
Leathered glove; narcotic clamps
Repressed footage on the floor
Crimson chains on flagellant

Reluctant head to glass reflect
From silken veil to sinews bare
Denuded ape in dumb address
No questions asked; no self to care

Rebecca Muir

OH COME SWEET BREEZE

Oh come sweet breeze and cool my brow
This warm and sunny day;
Just kiss my cheek and tease my hair
And blow my cares away.

Oh come sweet breeze envelop me
In heady scents of spring,
And set the meadow grass to dance
As lambs go gambolling.

Oh come sweet breeze and let the sounds
Of Nature reach my ears,
And when Earth's beauty makes me weep
Be there to dry my tears.

Oh come sweet breeze, forsake me not
When twilight dims the sky,
Just breathe amid the evening hush -
A whispered lullaby.

Diane Hemp

PRIZE POSSESSION

I watch the package empty
books and plastic

flowers, Russian tea cups
stained with wine,

a replica
of Frankenstein

in lace and pearls
and thyroid eyes,

covered over with dresses
discarded

summers and the ritual
of taking out

and placing
is too much

to retain, too much
to forget

what months may evolve
clean and sleeping

pressed tight to your chest.
Prised into life

where the eyes
tighten and shatter.

Ian Brook

THE OCEAN

I'm as deep as the ocean
And shallow enough to reach the shore.
I've got lots of wreckage hidden in my depths,
I'll make waves to get a whole lot more.
I surround little islands of beauty,
Sometimes I meet with the sky,
I reflect the images of Sun and Moon
- They control me - I don't know why
Gravity pulls me towards you,
My emotions remind you of tides.
With me you feel like you're drowning
My waves provide thousands of rides.
I can take the weight of a battleship,
You can insert a huge submarine.
It's your eyes that always remind me
Of the Ocean that I've always been.

Deborah

DOES HAPPINESS HAVE A SHAPE?

Such devastation feeds on feelings from within one's inner emotions,
Drinking the power into the body.
Not true power, but falsely found,
Giving no accusations, instead, camouflaged ideals.
Tempers as thin as snowflakes,
Words are bellowed from dishonest mouths, while candles are blown out.
Do we make such an effort to show we are shown as we should be?
Transparent layers glued together,
People hang pictures, illusions, in front of trueness.
We know not of what we see or hear,
But of what is not on show to outsiders.
Dare we be intimidated by such folk we see around us.
We are scared of what we do not know,
As we are not sure of what is right or wrong.
But we do what others think we should.
We are us.
Do nothing but explode
Explode into riots of spontaneous truths
Do we live for ourselves or for the manipulation of others?
It goes on forever.
What can I do, but watch myself fade away.

Barnaby Parsons

INSOMNIA

In the quiet hours of darkness
When I'm warm and safe in bed,
All is motionless and stillness,
Save the thoughts inside my head.

In the quiet hours of darkness
When all things are hid from sight,
Save the silver moon, the ebony,
And starlit studded night.

In the quiet hours of darkness
When there's nothing to be heard,
Save the deaf'ning sound of silence
To which naught can be compared.

In the quiet hours of darkness
All is resting; all is peace.
Yet my thoughts torment and tease me
And will give me no release.

In the quiet hours of darkness
Inconsolable I weep,
As I pray for blissful slumbers,
As I wait for blessed sleep.

Through the endless hours of darkness,
Just the moon and I awake.
Now the moon can sleep, for in the east
The dawn begins to break.

As the rising sun spreads lightness
So begins another day,
And the endless hours of darkness
Now, in silence, slip away.

Alison Gibbs

ELEGY

I wander in contemplative mood
Through crumbling, moss - clad tombstones
And think of times ahead:
Of those unborn whom I shall never know,
Of foreign places I shall never visit,
Lakes and mountains,
Noisy, sinister bazaars,
Of wondrous creatures awesome in their beauty,
Of curious customs of some primal tribe,
Of mist-wreathed suns and frosted stars,
And yellow moons that hang so low,
A breath might blow them out of orbit.
All the wonders that I long to know,
I'll see through your eyes, son,
I'll know through you.

L McGhee

SHADES

A guardian angel in disguise
Who boasts a pair of guiding eyes
That look beyond my body and face
To a deeper, darker, bleaker place.
He knows my mind inside out
Yet questions me all about
Things he knows *all* the answers to
Yet I'm mesmerised
What can I do?
He leads me out of this life
More romantic than using a knife
But then he flees with the morning
And leaves me with another day dawning.

Amanda Loh

A REST IS JUST A NIGHTMARE

I am afraid to sleep,
To close my eyes and rest,
The visions there will come again,
Inside my head infest,
They will torment me, in my dreams,
And laugh at me, and joke,
Then suddenly I will awake,
There in the sweat I'll soak.

Patrick Hannigan

THE BURIAL OF LILY OF AVALON

So Arthur's gift had come to be a personal parting,
In Camelot by one of the roving streams
That drifts along with sad tidings departing
On the journey to her home in far away dreams.
The King himself had dug her grave,
Finding under the laburnum tree a shady spot,
Her precious life he could not save,
He had owed her a wish and this is what she got.
Noble lords and ladies wept at this sight,
As dressed in yellow silk she had been laid to rest,
Even in death she was radiant and bright,
Her hands pressed with lilies at the King's request.
After the funeral had ended only Arthur remained,
And by the setting sun he kissed his sword and wept,
On one knee he knelt silently praying for his friend,
Until the sun of a new day above his castle crept.

G Saunders

REMEMBRANCE

Many feet have trod my path
And down my aisle sedately walked.
Ghostly echoes of hymns and sermons
Silent thoughts of those in prayer
Permeate my scarred and soot-stained walls
Though I am now a burned out relic
They linger on, in the smoke, dank air.

M Lewis

RHYTHMS OF THE MIND

Thrust into a world of isolation,
With the rhythms of life still abound,
Rejoicing in the splendour,
Of the shadows of the voices left in the mind,
Once the world was in sound,

Isolation is a mystery to the soul,
Turning deeds into visions,
When the picture was sold.

Music fills the soul with the impression of stars,
Dancing its way through the system,
Into our hearts.

Infinite visions,
No TV could make,
Whose pictures of images,
Pass through our lives,
Day to day.

Rhythms of music,
Spiralling the whispers of our dreams,
Into beautiful images in our minds' infinite cinema screen.

Niki Horvath

DAY

I wake to face another day of uncertainty. The sun shines through the window, warm on my face, lighting the room. Yet it is cold, dull, death looms, hanging in the air.

I pass the room where she lies dying. The reaper at her bedside, waiting for a chance to pluck her from existence.

I talk to him, ask him why her? Why wait? He looks at me haunting my soul, my very being, trying to kill me with his eyes, using them as his scythe.

Pale, thin, dying, I gaze at her, different from the woman I once knew, but could not place. In my heart I was dying with her.

She used to cradle me in her arms, chauffeur me around in a pram on a summer's day when life had meaning, vibrant colour. We were alive.

She never walked. She flowed. Her hair, a cascade of brown hair which synchronised life and meaning in unison. Her aura, her torch in the night.

She lies there now. Dead yet living, a lifeless shell free of soul, no longer on a plain of extant.

I wander around in a strange yet familiar land. Everyone to me is a stranger, naive to the torture I face. They laugh and joke and I yell why? Why? *Why?* When life is dead.

What do I do if she dies? Join her? Shall I shoot myself? I would feel no pain, my soul is dead. I would give up all for one minute longer with her.

She loses her grip on life. The reaper stands ready. Doctors educated philistinian poofs with BMW's rush in syringes ready. They hurt her, make her scream, yet they continue the torture.

I see him, I shout at him 'Take her now release her from her pain, release her, release us!'

I pull my gun. I stand there pointing the gun at him. There was I trying to kill death.
He turns to face me saying 'Her time has not yet come through, she will join me.'

The uncertainty becomes too much, pain, deep pain shooting through my body. I want to die. I turn the gun towards me, slowly drawing back the hammer. I look at her, dying, she looks back, smiles.

John Murphy

INFORMATION

We hope you have enjoyed reading this book - and that you will continue to enjoy it in the coming years.

If you like reading and writing poetry drop us a line, or give us a call, and we'll send you a free information pack.

Write to

        Poetry Now Information
        1-2 Wainman Road
        Woodston
        Peterborough
        PE2 7BU.